Unwin Education Books: 5

ORGANISING AND INTEGRATING THE INFANT DAY

Unwin Education Books

Series Editor: Ivor Morrish, BD, BA, DIP. ED. (London), BA (Bristol)

1. Education Since 1800 IVOR MORRISH
2. Moral Development WILLIAM KAY
3. Physical Education for Teaching BARBARA CHURCHER
4. The Background of Immigrant Children IVOR MORRISH
5. Organising and Integrating the Infant Day JOY TAYLOR

Unwin Education Books: 5
Series Editor: Ivor Morrish

Organising and Integrating the Infant Day

JOY TAYLOR

MA (Hons.)
Postgraduate Certificate in Education

Head of Education Department
The Lady Spencer-Churchill College of Education, Wheatley, Oxford.

London
GEORGE ALLEN AND UNWIN LTD
RUSKIN HOUSE MUSEUM STREET

First published in 1971
Second Impression 1972

ISBN 0 04 372001 3 cloth
0 04 372002 1 paper

Printed in Great Britain
in 11 point Times Roman
by Lowe & Brydone (Printers) Ltd, London

To Juliet and David

Acknowledgements

I am much indebted to my colleague, Miss Marian Brown, who read the manuscript and made many helpful suggestions; to Mrs Annemarie Porter, who typed it; and to all the children who will never know how much they have personally contributed to this book.

Contents

1. The Need for Organisation 11
2. The Organisation of the Classroom 15
3. The Use of Apparatus 24
4. The Organisation of the Traditional Daily Programme 34
5. Integration or Disintegration 51
6. The Transition from a Traditional Programme to an Integrated Day 58
7. Supplementary Organisation—Integrated and Traditional 79
8. The Organisation of School Classes 91
9. Team Teaching 101
10. Conclusion 109

Select Bibliography 113

Index 115

Chapter 1

The Need for Organisation

As the infant school has moved from the hushed formality of the past to the energetic scene of active participation we know today, the task of the teacher has in many ways become progressively more exacting. That the change has brought its rewards needs no underlining. Yet few people would deny that modern methods, by their very nature, have presented the infant teacher with a most rigorous and testing challenge to her professional skill and organising ability. While not seeking to diminish the effort of our forbears, faced with the exercise of instructing sixty or seventy children according to the rigid requirements of their day, many would agree that the task of controlling, organising and teaching thirty or forty active infants can be a daunting experience.

Perhaps it is legitimate, however, to suggest that it need not necessarily be so. New techniques need new managerial skills in any enterprise. But in the effort to develop and perfect the techniques, the importance of the managerial skills can be overlooked. The teacher can be equipped with a sound theoretical knowledge of how children learn and of how she should teach. She can faithfully provide the material her children need, and she can apply herself to creating a classroom environment with all the ingredients for teaching that is satisfying and for learning that should lead to success. She may have the interest, the patience and the will, and with the techniques at her fingertips she is entitled to embark upon her task with the hope that her effort will not be unrewarded.

There may, however, be an essential element missing from this catalogue of training and skill. This is the element of good, sound, well-considered organisation. The most effective material can fail in its application because the organisation behind its presentation is insecure and does not permit of its proper use. The most thoughtful plans can go inexplicably wrong because they are not adequately supported by an organisational framework in which they can function. And yet it is in this important area of management that there is often uncertainty and lack of clear direction. Many infant teachers are left to learn this particular skill in the hard school of experience, with all the strain and discouragement that can accompany them on the way.

Though nothing can replace the value of experience in consolidating theoretical knowledge, the experience itself is likely to be happier and more fruitful if it has a basis on which to build. The busy teacher, with daily charge of a lively class, often has little opportunity for considering then and there the answers to the organisational problems which constantly present themselves. The answers will undoubtedly emerge sooner or later, but if some of the frustrations can be minimised by an earlier consideration of the detail of class management there seems little reason to deny to the teacher this advantage.

It would be captious to suggest that the managerial skills of infant teaching are entirely neglected in training or in initial school experience. They are not. But among all the other pressing daily demands, these skills tend to be presented as random thoughts on the fringe of the techniques they support. Indeed, they may become fragmented and lost among the techniques, and the need remains for them to be drawn together and systematised so that they are available for the teacher's deliberate use. Little that will appear in these pages will be totally unfamiliar, even to the most inexperienced; but in identifying the detail of organisation and assembling it into a recognisable whole a useful purpose may perhaps be served. Organisation is important. It is acknowledged to be so. It is in extracting its elements in order to apply them that the difficulty sometimes lies.

If organisation is to be identified as a teaching element that needs specific consideration, some definition of its scope must be attempted. It begins where it should begin—in the classroom; and there it is the sum of many parts. A small detail of organisation can, in its own way, be as important as any of the larger issues. Just as one log can jam the whole pile, so a shaky piece of detailed organisation can cause difficulties out of all proportion to the time and effort required to eliminate the problem, once it has been identified. Thus it is true to say that in organisation detail is never to be despised, because when all the minutes have been saved and a sufficient number of minor frustrations avoided the total relief to the teacher can be considerable.

Therefore organisation in the classroom deserves attention, and this includes organisation of the room itself, of materials and equipment, of the children's work and play (if, indeed, the two can be distinguished), and of teaching techniques and methods. All this can take time, but it is time profitably invested. It is amply repaid by the subsequent economy of effort, of physical and nervous energy and of repetitive attention to the daily minutiae of classroom life. And the ultimate saving of time that can be devoted to more profitable occupation is a dividend well worth having.

Organisation, of course, extends beyond the walls of the individual classroom. There are different ways in which the classes in a school may be organised, from a fairly traditional though often fluid daily programme to a partially or fully integrated day. This may sometimes be extended to include varying degrees of co-operative or team teaching. Again, there is variety in the age structure of classes, which may be organised on the basis of the single-age group, the family group or the parallel group.

These matters are usually, though not invariably, governed by school policy, but it falls to the individual teacher to organise her class accordingly. Consideration must therefore be given to the organisation which these developments necessitate, because difficulties can arise if the pattern which fits one system is superimposed upon another. Here again a good deal may be left to pragmatic effort, and the tentative period while teacher and children are feeling their way into a new situation can be harassing and frustrating for both. To some extent this can be alleviated by identifying the organisational problems and considering ways in which they might be overcome.

Amid all the uncertainties of the changing pattern of infant school organisation, two things, which are not unconnected, remain constant and beyond doubt. One is that the quality and the skill of the individual teacher outweigh all else in determining the success of her organisation. And the other is that there is certainly no blueprint for successful organisation, no single, foolproof system guaranteed to work in all circumstances with every teacher, and every child, in every school. All that can be said is that there are certain common problems, identifiable, and often responsive to a systematic approach; but the degree to which the individual teacher seeks to apply any common remedies will be governed by her own particular classroom situation. It is upon her own skill and flexibility in adapting and applying the remedies that the success of her organisation will ultimately depend.

Chapter 2

The Organisation of the Classroom

Irrespective of the broad organisational policy adopted by an individual school or class, the details of classroom organisation and management need careful thought if they are to contribute significantly to the smooth running of the teacher's and the children's day. However, it is as well to recognise from the outset that organisation can never be an end in itself. One of the fundamental principles on which it should be based is that it must, essentially, be the servant and not the master. It must support the purposes of learning and teaching, not dictate them. It is therefore worth identifying these purposes before examining the organisational structure which might contribute to their fulfilment.

Fortunately the teacher's and the children's purposes here are not in conflict. They meet on common ground, and if the teacher's aims and interests are met so also will be the children's. To summarise what every infant teacher knows, it is broadly true to say that at the heart of the aims of modern methods lie the progress and the well-being, not only of the class as a whole, but also of each child within it. This requires, on the teacher's part, an organisation which specifically caters for the individual, multiplied by every child in the class. And on the child's part, the requirement is that he, the individual, can recognise and comprehend the organisation, can conduct himself within it so that his need for activity and participation is met, and yet can share the attention and the resources of his teacher with many others whose needs are similar to his own.

Organisation within the classroom should, and undoubtedly can, help to realise these aims. For the teacher to be able to cater for the individual child within the class, her overwhelming need is for time—and her organisation can help to provide a little more of this for her. It must free her, as far as is possible, from routine chores like giving out materials and apparatus that children could find for themselves; it must help to reduce interruptions of the 'I've-finished-what-shall-I-do-now?' variety; it must enable her to undertake group or individual teaching without her attention being too much diverted by the needs of other children; it must make possible the establishment of a known routine in innumerable small ways, so that these things demand no more than passing attention to keep them going.

A vital element in this time-saving exercise is delegation, an expedient sometimes overlooked by a busy teacher with nobody to whom she can delegate except the comparatively unorganised and unskilled occupants of her reception classroom. The opportunities for delegation are, to be sure, much more limited here than they are when six- or seven-year-olds are available, but they are not entirely absent. Even in his first term in school Jimmy is capable of getting his own scissors, provided that (*a*) he really wants to use them, (*b*) he knows where they are, and (*c*) he also knows that nobody else will get them for him if he does not do so. This may be a primitive form of 'delegation' but it represents, among other things, a unit of time—which Jimmy instead of the teacher spends in fetching the scissors.

It also represents much else. This function of Jimmy's is part of a much wider issue, and one which is educationally sound. It is the beginning of his school training in the development of his initiative, his independence and his personal responsibility for some of the things he does. It is largely this development which enables him to make greater use of opportunities to pursue his own interests and to learn from his own activity, without occupying a disproportionate share of his teacher's attention. This is part of the common ground on which the teacher's and the child's interests meet. Both can benefit from conscious delegation, gradually extended as the opportunities increase and the training begins to take effect.

However, this does not necessarily happen automatically. Indeed, it hardly needs to be said that the child is not unknown who stretches the teacher to the limits of her patience and tenacity if she is to cause it to happen at all! Despite all the theory, Jimmy will not always fetch his own scissors and Mary will not always feel obliged to remain obediently at her tracing because good organisation and the needs of other children require that they should do so. But this is not to say that deliberate training and a sound organisational structure do not make it possible for some of these desirable things to happen some of the time. It can even come about—with good fortune and a favourable wind behind—that the teacher's efforts in this direction will be quite richly rewarded. It is therefore worth examining some of the detail of organisation which may help to bring these splendid horizons somewhere near the reality of the classroom floor.

The organisation of the room space in which one teaches is a subject fraught with danger for the idealists. There are few things more irritating to the teacher working in cramped and difficult conditions than well-meaning advice based on unrealistic assumptions. All classrooms are not modern, spacious and amply fitted with cupboards and worktops. It is unfortunately a fact that so often the teacher must compromise, adjusting her sights to keep within the boundaries of reality and accepting the physical limitations that no amount of goodwill can overcome.

However, there is no reason why one should not at least reflect upon the ideal situation, and try to come as near to it as conditions will allow. And even in the most unpromising circumstances it is worth examining any possibilities which may help to alleviate a difficulty or two.

Where space is a severe problem, it may be helpful to take a new look at the situation and see whether there is anything at all that can be dispensed with in order to make more room. Essentially this exercise is a matter of looking at priorities, and of seriously considering whether some things which have long been automatically placed at the top of the list could not in fact be moved further down. For example, is a table and chair for every child *really* necessary, if choices have to be made?

There is no doubt whatever that the child who has always had his own table and chair can become really upset if he finds himself unexpectedly deprived of them. To him, his accustomed place in the classroom is his personal estate, and it is occupied by someone else only as a great favour and with a strict understanding of the temporary nature of the arrangement. But despite all this, an alternative is not, from the child's point of view, impossible. If the teacher prepares the children for a change in the familiar pattern, taking them into her confidence as 'colleagues' jointly planning a mutually beneficial operation, it is surprising how far the children will go in co-operating with the scheme. It is the unexpected deprivation of a child's place which disturbs him, especially when nobody else appears to have been similarly dispossessed. It is therefore essential that if changes are to be made with children who are accustomed to the traditional pattern they should be fully prepared beforehand and have taken part in the planning of the whole enterprise.

If, then, the children can be persuaded of the benefits of removing some of the furniture, how is the teacher to organise the class with what remains? And what exactly should remain? To take the second question first, the list (excluding equipment such as Wendy House, book-corner unit, etc.) might be:

(*a*) Enough tables and chairs for use in the traditional way by about half the class at a time. If other suitable work-tops are available to double up for this purpose, the number of tables retained can be correspondingly reduced.

(*b*) Enough chairs *somewhere* in the room to enable every child to sit down if he so wishes.

(*c*) Units containing small drawers so that each child has one of his own. This is particularly important if he is no longer to have his own 'place', and if drawer units are not available something else must be retained to take personal tidy-boxes or bags.

(*d*) As many cupboards as space will allow.

(*e*) A chair for the teacher and a desk if she wants it.

(*f*) A table for each working bay that can now be accommodated in the space vacated by superfluous individual tables.

Every teacher will no doubt wish to add one or two items to this list, according to her personal preference and within the limitations imposed by her particular classroom.

Turning now to the question of organising a class where there is no longer a permanent place for each child, it is as well to begin by considering how these places (especially the tables) are normally used. They are in essential use when all the class is required to undertake certain activities at the same time, i.e. when the children are making the kind of things for which they need a working surface at table height, or when they are doing some form of continuous written recording. The places are not, for example, necessarily used by the children who are measuring cupboards, tables, etc. around the room; for their recording is in the form of brief jottings in the intervals of taking measurements and this can conveniently be done on a corner of the window-sill or the top of a locker.

It is therefore worth reflecting upon the extent to which it is really essential for all the children to use tables simultaneously. Even assuming a fairly traditional timetable, is it not possible to arrange a programme so that only half the children are recording at their tables, while the others are engaged on activities that do not really require tables at all? Could they not be busy with sorting trays on the floor, with weighing, measuring, shopping or practical apparatus for which a table is not essential? In activity time, can just half the class make potato prints, while the other half is painting, building, dressing up and playing in the Wendy House?

The answer to these questions is almost certainly 'yes'; and the vast majority of teachers, even if they are operating a comparatively traditional programme, do not in any case organise their classes on lines more formal than these. If one really examines the pattern in most infant classrooms, one finds that for the greater part of the day many of the tables are not in indispensable use, even though they are there. So perhaps it is not quite as big a step as it seems to get rid of some of them altogether and transfer a few others to different purposes. If it is quite impossible to store them elsewhere, then the battle is, regrettably, lost before it is joined. But let us not accept total defeat while any possibility of victory remains.

However, even when this re-arrangement is practicable it does not necessarily produce *more* floor space; but it does permit of its use in a different and more flexible way. It makes possible, for example, an arrangement of 'bays' and 'corners' for working areas, which have considerable educational advantages besides making organisation in many ways simpler. These bays may be devised by placing cupboards and lockers at right angles to the wall and making use of their backs as display areas. Alternatively, the large rolls of coloured corrugated cardboard now on the market are most effective for this purpose.

Where space is not an outstanding problem, it is correspondingly easier to make use of bays. Their number will, however, be limited by space in any classroom, and the teacher's choice of those she will have will depend upon her own priorities. But her general organisation will, without doubt, benefit noticeably if the bays are planned and equipped as well as conditions allow.

A mathematics bay, for example, is invaluable. This should accommodate as much mathematics material as possible—partly with a view to organisational advantages. For instance, if the rulers are here rather than in a less accessible place, children are more likely to help themselves instead of depending upon the teacher to provide them. If there is room for a shop, it is convenient to have it adjacent to the weighing table. The balances or scales can then be common to both, thus eliminating unnecessary movement across the room by shoppers who need to weigh. It is this kind of attention to detail which really helps. The object is not to restrict children's movement, but to give generally greater freedom of movement by reducing that which is unproductive.

A painting or 'art' corner is well worth considering. If space permits, a table on which a variety of creative materials is provided is a genuine incentive for children to experiment with them. The very fact that the materials are visible and accessible helps with ideas and encourages some children to try them out. Ideally, this area should be somewhere near the sink, if there is one, so that it is easier to insist upon children washing their own brushes and water jars when they have finished, and putting them away. This kind of 'self-help' (or delegation), multiplied many times, really does provide the teacher with some of the extra minutes which she can so valuably use.

There is everything to be said for a reading or 'quiet' bay, however great the limitation which space puts upon its size. 'Quiet', of course, means all things to all infants, and it is not suggested that a 'silence' rule should be imposed upon an enclave surrounded by more turbulent territory. But it is perfectly reasonable to assume that the quiet bay is where people go to relax (as even infants can), comfortably and preferably with a bit of carpet on the floor. This is not an alarmist suggestion designed to incite revolution among the taxpayers. It is not, in fact, an expensive one. Quite large samples of discontinued range carpets can be obtained at little or no cost, and when sewn together make excellent library corner carpets.

Carpets do, quite seriously, help to create the right atmosphere in a small part of the room where atmosphere matters. They add a touch of luxury and a certain air of desirability to a place where you look at books—you even look at them just for pleasure, without the *quid pro quo* that you must find something out. You are not obliged to be silent, but if you want to be energetic you must go somewhere else. And with a good selection of attractively produced books, arranged and displayed so that they ask to be looked at, the quiet corner has a value out of all proportion to the time it takes to provide it.

Every teacher will have her own ideas about the bays she wishes to have, and it would be tedious to dwell upon thoughts concerning half a dozen. But the question does arise, inevitably: What is the point of going to all this trouble to have corners or bays at all? What are their advantages over the traditionally arranged classroom, or is this just another example of trying something else merely for the sake of it?

The answer must be that there is real purpose in this development. The organisation which the bay makes possible does have advantages, and it is far from being a question of change just for the sake of it. It is probably true to say that a system of organisation based on bays is a logical result of developments in teaching techniques, an instance of the support which organisation must give to the purposes of learning and teaching. It is when the organisational framework lags behind and fails to give this support that the structure can begin to show signs of weakness.

Basically, the change in teaching technique which has come

about over the last twenty years or so has been the increasing emphasis on the individual or small group approach. This was certainly not new twenty years ago, but it has become more widespread and explicit for several reasons and its effects on day-to-day classroom routine are important. Not the least of these effects stem from the increasing demands on the teacher's time, on the child's capacity to be resourceful—and on room space.

We may take one possible example. A number of different activities—or similar activities at different levels—are to be undertaken during a given period of time. Two children will need to use rulers and measuring cards, another requires the box of shapes, three are to work on a model, a small group is to use pre-reading apparatus and one sturdy character wants the magnifying glass, the book about beetles and the 'specimens' he brought in a box which is on the nature table. It is neither possible nor profitable for the teacher to hand out this variety of material. There are some twenty-five other children in the class, four of whom need about ten minutes of her main attention for the direct teaching of phonics that is due to them. She *must* be able to delegate the task of acquiring the materials to the children who are going to use them.

However, if they are to be able to discharge the responsibilities of this delegation without fuss and confusion, children must be accustomed to an organisation which enables—and expects—them to do so. They must know where the materials are, and this assumes a permanent place where things are normally to be found. Furthermore, if the book about beetles is in the same place as the books which a good many other children want, or if the rulers, the measuring cards, the pre-reading apparatus and the box of shapes are all in one cupboard, too many bodies will converge simultaneously upon the same place. Worse still, if children have to wander about looking for rulers and scissors and clock faces which have strayed because they have no recognisable home, class control will deteriorate and the teacher's time and energy be dissipated.

It is, of course, perfectly possible to overcome these problems without the use of bays. They do, however, help to simplify the operation. They effectively spread the children round the room, according to the activities and interests they are pursuing, and this is as good a way as any of achieving maximum use of space. Because they concentrate related material in certain areas, they make it easier for children to find what they want. Books on different topics can be displayed in their bays instead of all being in one place; it is then more likely that children concerned with that topic will find and use them. Bays stimulate discussion among those who are following similar interests, and they tend to draw children to them and awaken their curiosity because they have a certain identity and separation from the rest of the room. These are solid advantages, which make a really noticeable contribution to the organisation of a class geared to individual and small group teaching methods.

Cupboard space in the classroom needs to be most carefully planned. Those which are accessible to children should, as far as possible, be allocated to the materials they are expected to find and use. Nobody will pretend that because the counters are kept on a particular shelf all children will at all times dutifully return them after use to their appointed place. Neither will the teacher always escape the question 'Where are the counters?'. Paul knows perfectly well where they are, and he asks the question more for attention and social contact than for information. There is nothing reprehensible about this. Indeed, attention and social contact with his teacher are a very necessary part of Paul's life. But she can give them to him in many more profitable ways if her time is not too much occupied in answering routine questions to which children already know the answers. In any case, it is better for Paul to be independent in the matter of finding his counters.

It takes training and insistence for delegation to work. Even then, it will not work every time. It is fortunate that this is so, since children are children and no one wants them to be perfect little cogs on beautifully oiled wheels. However, we need not be too serious about this. There is little danger of the good teacher organising for perfection. She tries to strike a commonsense balance between the 'system' and the child, and the extent to which she achieves this is one measure of her success.

Chapter 3

The Use of Apparatus

Apparatus justifies its inclusion in a book about organisation because it is an excellent vehicle for delegation if it is well designed and systematically provided. In this context, the word refers specifically to card apparatus and not to the practical material normally included in the general term. (The use of the latter is, of course, taken for granted.)

The 'assignment' method is one which is widely adopted in infant schools in order to make individual teaching possible with an extensive ability range and quite often the full age range as well. Sometimes, and particularly when children can read with some fluency, commercially produced work-books and cards can be profitably used. But one has to accept that they do leave many gaps. This is unavoidable, since they have to be designed for very general application and they cannot take account of the particular needs and rate of progress of each separate child. Neither can they take account of the different materials available in every classroom or of the limitation on the words which the beginner can read since these vary according to the scheme or method by which he is being taught. The teacher, on the other hand, is in a position to take account of all these variables, and to design her material with particular reference to Tommy in Class 4.

However, if part of the function of apparatus is to make delegation easier and thereby to contribute to class organisation, it has to be planned in a rather more systematic manner than is necessary if it is to be used entirely as a teaching aid. It is with this objective in view that apparatus is discussed in this chapter, and the individual teacher will interpret the discussion according to the circumstances of her classroom, her children and her own teaching techniques.

Apparatus of this kind falls, broadly, into three categories:

(i) That which gives the child an instruction to do something, which the teacher could give him personally if she had the time, e.g. 'measure your shoe'.

(ii) That which helps the child to learn a certain process, e.g. word-matching.

(iii) That which gives the child practice in a particular process, e.g. sum cards. Practice is unlikely to do much to *bring about* understanding of the process, but it has value in consolidating and reinforcing the understanding once it has come from practical experience.

Card apparatus which does not fall into one of these categories will not particularly help organisation, although it may have value for some other purpose. However, it is very time-consuming to make, and it is always worth considering carefully its proposed objective in order to have some certainty that the exercise is justified.

There are certain requirements which good apparatus must meet if it is to be of maximum value.

1. It must do what it is intended to do

If, for example, it is the teacher's intention that a piece of apparatus should help to reinforce a child's understanding of number values, she might design it something like this:

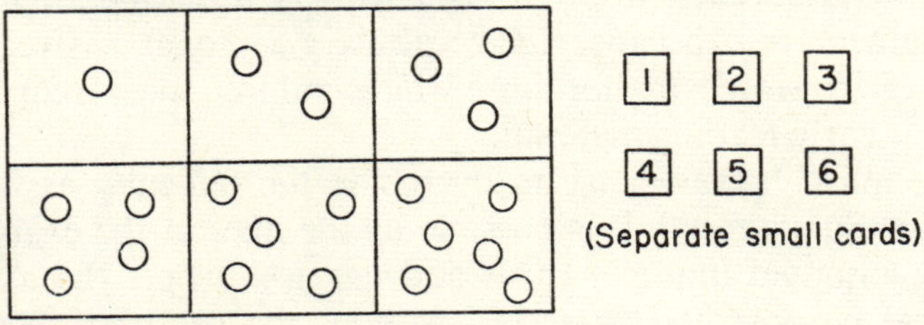

Or she might be misled (regrettably all too often by beautifully produced work-books) into doing this:

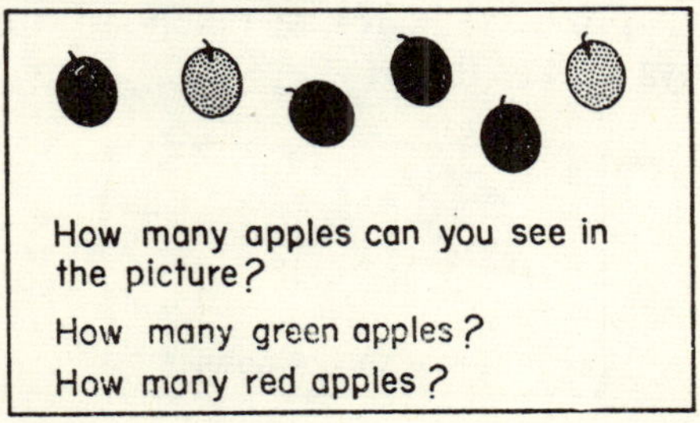

The first of these examples is clear, simple in operation, requires no reading ability, and achieves precisely what it is intended to achieve—the reinforcement of the child's understanding of number values (given, of course, the normal development this piece of apparatus would have in the teaching situation). The same purpose would also be served with, for instance, a number jigsaw made from manilla.

The second example is, however, virtually useless for its intended purpose. If the child is still at the stage when reinforcement of his number values to six is necessary, his reading ability will most certainly not be sufficient to enable him to get anywhere near the mathematics on this card. If the purpose of the card were to give the child practice in reading, it might have some minimal value (minimal, because if this were the aim there are much better ways of doing it). And if the teacher has to read the card for him every time in order to enable him to do the mathematics it does not help her with delegation at all.

2. It must take account of the child's reading and writing ability in the early stages

This requirement follows automatically from the first, and it is by no means easy to satisfy. The problem applies particularly to mathematics, because its vocabulary is so extensive; and most of the words are not those which children meet frequently in their early reading material.

We must, however, try to overcome the difficulty as far as we can. Sometimes this is possible on the lines of the examples already quoted (number cards and jigsaws), where the mathematical purpose can be served without the need for reading. However, it is not always possible, or even desirable, to abolish words altogether. Words can be used judiciously to help reading along, provided care is taken to minimise their difficulty in ways such as these:

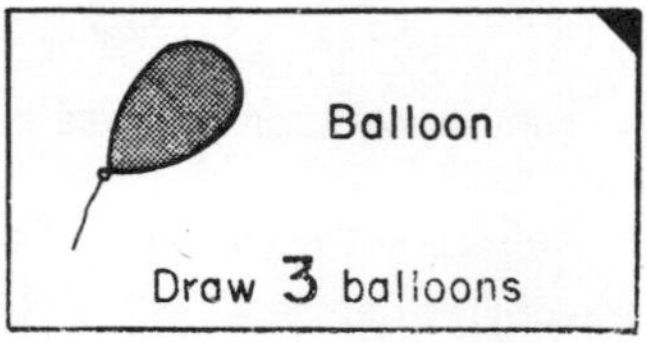

(*a*) Use a coloured border or symbol or distinguishing mark of some kind, and illustrate the nouns (see drawing on p.26). The first few times that Anne uses a card like this she will have to ask the teacher, or a more advanced child, what it says. But there is so little writing on it that to read it to her will be literally a momentary task. And with explanation and training she will learn that the cards with red corners all ask her to draw the object that is illustrated on them, and the number of objects to be drawn is indicated by the red figure. (Children can usually decipher the figure before they can read the full written word.) A system such as this does not eliminate reference to the teacher for help with reading, but it does considerably reduce it.

(*b*) Keep the number of words on a card or set of cards to the absolute minimum, make the form of words as repetitive as possible, and illustrate the nouns, e.g. (i) below in preference to (ii).

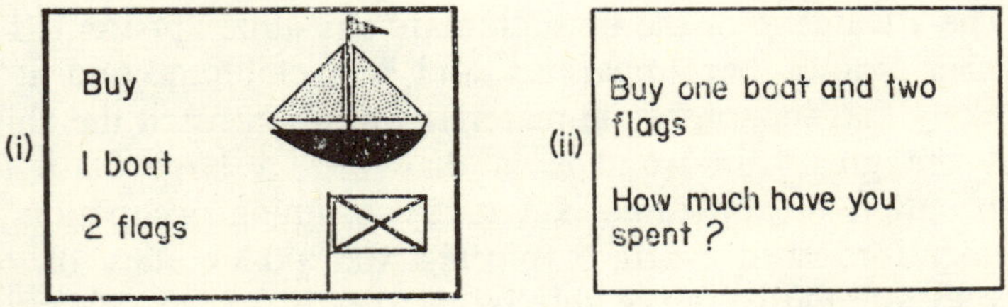

With (i) the addition required will be presented as part of the assignment when these cards (with red borders) are first introduced. Those at a later stage, involving change and subtraction, will have green borders. There is therefore no need to write this instruction on the card.

(*c*) By means of flash cards, wall charts, etc., do some direct teaching of common words and phrases used in mathematics, e.g. measure, weigh, buy, how many, balance, etc.

With regard to the question of children recording their work from assignment cards, again particularly with mathematics, this requirement should be minimal in the early stages. Sometimes it is possible for oral and practical recording to suffice. But if written recording is necessary it should be accepted in the briefest form. When writing is still rather slow and laborious, the enjoyment and the value of the mathematical experience may well be diminished by too great a demand for words. If the cost of one boat and two flags is 5p, then all the child should be asked to record is '5p', without any verbal additions such as 'I have spent'. Opportunities for writing come when this is the object of the exercise, and the content of the material will then be purpose-designed. So with written recording, as with reading, care should be taken to relate assignment work to the child's ability at that stage.

3. It must be designed in stages and recognisably graded
Accepting that with individual and group teaching methods a considerable range of apparatus must be provided, the teacher has to devise some means of ensuring that within this range the material matches the child. There are, in effect, only two ways of doing this. One is for the teacher to distribute the apparatus on every occasion; and the other is for each child to be in a position to get his own.

The advantage of the first alternative is quite apparent. The teacher knows her apparatus and her children, and it is unlikely that inappropriate material will often reach the child. But the great disadvantage is that with a large class the distribution of apparatus is a time-consuming occupation. It is therefore well worth exploring the possibilities of the second alternative, since this is an area in which delegation might well be practicable.

Irrespective of organisation, apparatus must be designed in stages; since without this there is no systematic progression. If, however, the children are to be given the responsibility of helping themselves to their own apparatus they, as well as the teacher, must be able to recognise the stages that apply to them. Otherwise a child may find himself in possession of a card intended for a stage beyond that which he has reached, and because he cannot do it he will become bored or discouraged or both. Or he may take a card which is rather too easy, and even if he has no objection to this he will be wasting his time.

One of the simplest ways of enabling the child to recognise the stages is to relate them to colour. The stage one shopping cards might be the blue ones with red borders, and stage two those with green borders. With apparatus provided for a wide ability range, this means a considerable variety of colours, borders and so on. However, this does not present a great problem to the child, because he does not need to carry in his head more than the limited number of colour combinations that apply to him in any one stage. When he no longer needs one set, he is told which cards to do next. And if a system such as this is in operation, it is remarkable how quickly the children become familiar with the distinctions and can give each other the information if anyone is unsure.

It is rather less easy for the teacher. There is no problem if she is starting from scratch, since she can design a system and provide within it. But most teachers are not in that position, and it would hardly be realistic to expect them to discard all their material in order to institute a new system in the interests of organisation. However, again the problem is not insurmountable. If she designs a scheme of colours and distinguishing marks towards which she will work, any new apparatus and all replacements can be consistent with this scheme. If it is simply a matter of adding a coloured corner or border, this can quite quickly be done to existing cards. Some can be left untouched because the possibility of confusion is remote. There is little likelihood, for example, of the child who has reached the stage of being a reasonably fluent reader helping himself to the pre-reading matching apparatus, or vice versa.

There may still, however, be a fairly large proportion of apparatus which needs some kind of temporary means of distinction, at least until it reaches the end of its useful life. This might be dealt with by adding stars or some other symbol —one for the first stage, two for the next, and so on. Or they may be kept in a certain wall pocket, known to the children to whom these cards apply. A plan of this kind will take time to institute in the first place, and to make the children familiar with it. But once it is established, it really pays off. The chore of distribution becomes a thing of the past. The children can, and they do, take it over.

However, let us not be guilty of over-simplifying this step. The children will take over the chore only if the teacher deliberately and intentionally trains them to do so. Even then, they will not all accept this training without demur. Some will go on asking which card they should do long after they are perfectly familiar with the answer. But this is not a disaster. They will eventually accept the inevitable, with very good humour if their relationship with the teacher is a happy one. And the sympathetic teacher will always be aware of the timid child, who hesitates to commit himself in case he is wrong. She will continue to give him the reassurance of helping him to find the right card until he has enough confidence to depend upon himself.

There is one reservation to add to the use of a systematically graded scheme. It must, however efficiently designed, be administered with flexibility. If Tony is required to make his way doggedly through every card in a set, irrespective of the fact that by the time he reaches card 4 his understanding is fully consolidated, he will rebel against the yoke of the remaining six which stand between him and further progress. On the other hand, if Stephen is still on shaky ground when he has completed them all, he will not approach the next set with confidence, because the pace for him is too rapid. Tony must be permitted the short cuts, and extra provision made for Stephen. It is this kind of flexibility which makes the best of a well-designed and successfully administered grading system.

4. Accessibility

It goes without saying that if children are to help themselves to their own apparatus, it must be accessible to them. But this is not always very easy to arrange, especially in overcrowded conditions. However, delegation in the distribution of apparatus will break down if the problem of accessibility is impossible of solution, and it is worth exploring every possibility before abandoning the idea.

Wall pockets offer the most promising line of approach. These can be made quite quickly from manilla, and though they are not as durable as strong cotton ones their life is much longer than one might think. A set of three pockets can be made as follows:

Materials required: a piece of manilla 50 cm × 40 cm and 4 small pieces for gussets each 15 cm × 5 cm; glue; a roll of coloured insulating tape for strengthening edges (optional).

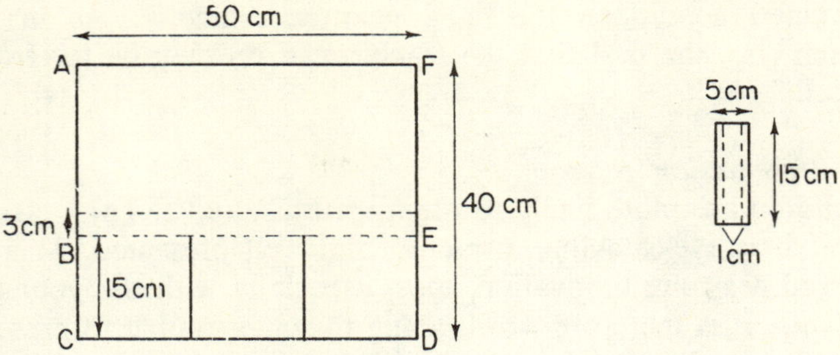

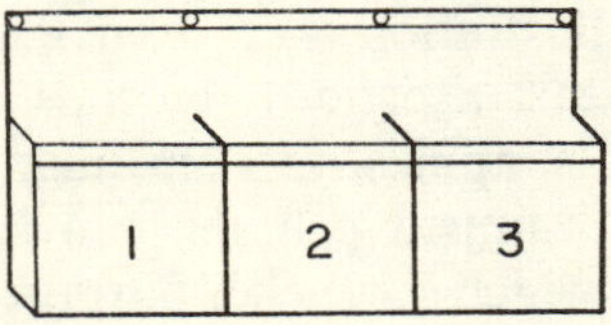

1. Fold along all dotted lines.
2. Rule guide lines from CD to BE as shown.
3. Strengthen edge AF and the outside of CD with insulating tape if required.
4. Glue the 1 cm fold on one side of each gusset, and stick the gussets along the edges BC and ED and on the guide lines.
5. Glue the other 1 cm fold of each gusset.
6. Fold CD over and stick gussets to back of wall pockets.
7. Punch pin holes along AF.

If there is enough pinboard to accommodate the pockets at child height, there is no accessibility problem. If not, ingenious measures are required. If anyone can be persuaded to fix a narrow strip of wood along a wall, this is sufficient to take some pockets. If there are any bays formed by protruding lockers or bookcases, the backs of these are ideal for the purpose. Even the sides of cupboards can be pressed into emergency use for small sets of pockets, and it is not unknown to find them fixed to the edges of window-sills or the outside of the Wendy House. One way or another it pays to find somewhere to put at least a few wall pockets, though in really cramped conditions this is a genuine difficulty. As in so much else, the best that the teacher can do may be far from ideal.

5. Presentation

Children are more likely to use apparatus, and to enjoy using it, if it is eye-catching, attractive and well presented. This is indeed a strong motivation, most especially with the younger infants. It is therefore worth going to some trouble to present it well. A coloured edge, in addition to being useful for reasons of organisation, can transform a fairly ordinary looking card into one which a young child feels drawn to use. So can an attractive illustration, and even the teacher who feels herself to be the least artistic of mortals can manage simple shapes such as balls, apples, fish and many more. With the aid of a coloured felt-tipped pen she can have a perfectly acceptable illustration which serves her purpose.

Ideally, cards should be covered in 'Contact', but unfortunately it is very expensive. It does, however, prolong the life of a card almost indefinitely, and it may not cost more in the long run because replacement is far less frequent. In terms of the teacher's time, the saving is well worth the extra money. So if the school is in a position to provide 'Contact' for at least some of the card apparatus, the teacher will feel that the time spent on designing and making really good material is more justified. A high standard of presentation is important enough for it to be taken into consideration when counting the cost.

6. Wall charts

A reference to wall charts might conveniently be made under the general heading of 'apparatus'. Some of them have a part to play in the encouragement of 'self-help', and to this extent their inclusion in a review of organisation is justified.

One of the main sources of distraction to the teacher engaged in individual or small group work is the constant stream of hopeful characters in need of words for their writing. The 'word queue' can sometimes threaten to become almost a permanent feature of the classroom scenery, and is one of the most difficult to abolish. The problem is intensified if the system of organisation in operation is one in which a number of children do their writing at the same time.

Wall charts can do something to help. Most teachers in any case make good use of the familiar and well-tried charts of colours, days of the week, the family, etc. But it is not so easy with the common everyday words which cannot be illustrated and which are in constant demand, words like 'yesterday' and 'brought'. Every teacher could immediately compile a list of these, which she seems to be forever having to write in somebody's word-book.

A list of these words on a chart is unhelpful because the child needs a clue to assist him with identification. An alternative is to make a chart of different coloured balloons, with a word in each; and the teacher (with benefit of tenacity) trains the children to remember that 'brought' is the word in the yellow balloon. They can then find it for themselves—most of the time. A wall of different coloured bricks or a skeleton tree with a few large coloured leaves will serve the same purpose and give variety. A chart of this description with the common words needed for mathematics might be situated in the mathematics bay and will ultimately help with reading the work cards.

A few odd minutes here and there are valuably spent in drawing children's attention to the words on the charts in order to gain the advantage of real familiarity. This, together with insistence on children finding the words for themselves instead of asking for them to be written in their word-books will make a positive contribution to reducing the length of the word queue. Charts of this kind do not represent a very major step forward in organisation. The point is only a small one; but many small points added together can be noticeably helpful in lessening routine demands on the teacher's time.

Chapter 4

The Organisation of the Traditional Daily Programme

Many infant schools are organised on the basis of a familiar and recognisably structured day, when certain activities take place at given times according to a programme devised by the teacher. The structure normally has the flexibility essential to modern teaching methods, and the good teacher takes full account of individual needs and interests to adjust her plans as the occasion presents itself. The form of organisation which, for various reasons, is expressly designed to give the *child* a greater degree of choice, i.e. that which has generally come to be known as the 'Integrated Day', will be discussed in later chapters. But first we will turn to the more traditionally structured programme and see how organisation may be used to support and strengthen the teacher's work.

It is probably true to say that in a pattern of this kind more time is allocated to the '3 Rs' than to any other separately identifiable activity. There may well be more time given in the course of the day to all the other activities together, which for convenience appear under different labels, e.g. 'nature', 'creative activities', 'story', etc. However, that which is officially designated as time for '3 Rs' is likely to be greater than any one of the others; and it is also likely to present the teacher with rather more pressing problems because of the nature and the variety of the ground to be covered. It follows that the detailed organisation of this period should be given especially careful attention.

It is not by chance that the more general title '3 Rs' has largely replaced the finer distinctions of 'reading', 'writing' and 'number' which used to be very familiar on the timetable. As our approach to teaching various 'subjects' changes it becomes progressively more difficult—and less desirable—to maintain artificial boundaries between them. Mathematics is no longer considered to be a branch of learning entirely separate from language; nor is 'writing' confined to 'stories' or the beginnings of literary composition. Still less can 'reading' be isolated as an end in itself, unrelated to much else that goes on in the normal course of the day. The 3 Rs have therefore come to be more broadly based and much less restrictive than they were when the phrase was originally coined.

This is very far from supporting the view that the components of the 3 Rs—or, indeed, any other 'subject'—are not in themselves legitimate studies, and it is most important that this should be explicitly stated. There is very little more damaging to a true understanding of, say, mathematics than to deprive it of its right to be logically and systematically developed along its own progressively designed course. Crossing boundaries does not mean that there is no territory between them to be explored and no heights to be scaled. It means only that artificial barriers to exploration should be removed. To go further than this is to create an insipid kind of no man's land, in which nothing is learned or taught except that which is quite fortuitously encountered on the way.

Accepting, then, that the components of the 3 Rs must still be taught (but in a mutually supportive framework), the question arises of how this fairly long period of time can be organised so that it is profitable to the children and practicable for the teacher. All that has been said about delegation, the use of apparatus and the organisation of the classroom will contribute something to the effective use of this time. But more detailed planning is necessary if the full value of the 3R period is to be realised.

Let us assume that the teacher has a class of thirty-five children, spanning about a year in age and with the full range of ability. (Family grouping will be considered in a later chapter.) The 3R period lasts for an hour, and there is probably another part of the day of perhaps half an hour or so when similar activities take place. This shorter period presents fewer organisational problems but the longer one has to be carefully planned if the children's effort and interest are to be sustained.

There are certain considerations, some essential and some open to choice, which have a direct bearing on the successful organisation of this longer period. They are:

1. Grouping

From an organisational point of view, grouping the children is not really a matter of choice. It is virtually essential. It is entirely a matter of the teacher's personal preference whether her children work together in a common or in a mixed ability grouping pattern. Some prefer one arrangement, some the other. On the one hand, if children of similar ability and attainment work together they can benefit from mutual discussion and interchange of ideas and information. It is sometimes easier, particularly for the inexperienced teacher, to have the 'red group' together as a coherent unit, for purposes of explanation, discussion and allocation of tasks. On the other hand, the great advantage of a mixed ability grouping pattern is that there are advanced children immediately available to give incidental help to the others, and provided this is not allowed to become troublesome to those who are further ahead it can be of great help to the busy teacher with a large class.

However, the point at issue is not the *fact* of grouping. For organisational purposes, the children in the 'red group' really do need to be of roughly comparable ability and attainment, at least for some of their activities. They do not, however, need to sit at the same table, unless the teacher wishes them to do so. As long as all the children know their groups, the teacher can allocate tasks to each group irrespective of where the children who belong to it are sitting. If the classroom arrangement is one in which each child does not have a permanent place, the 'red table' and the 'blue table' in any case cease to exist as established units. But if the teacher is to be able to organise her class so that the 'yellow group' is to begin the period with, for example, sorting trays, she must be in a position to assume that the children in that group are all at the stage when this activity is appropriate.

Grouping, therefore, is very necessary for organisational reasons; but, as already indicated, whether or not the teacher locates the children together in a common ability pattern or spreads them around in a mixed ability pattern is for her to decide. She should be able to make whichever arrangement she personally finds more satisfactory and easier to handle.

2. Span of concentration

There is a limit to the length of time for which people of any age can really concentrate on one particular task, and with young children this limit can be quickly reached. One cannot expect to be precise about exactly when this will happen. A child's span of concentration is governed by so many factors, such as maturity, interest, temperament, mood, physical comfort, etc. However, the teacher needs some kind of yardstick on which to base her planning, and as a very rough and ready guide the limit might be estimated as a maximum of about fifteen minutes for the youngest or least able to something like forty minutes at the top of the infant school. Every teacher is well acquainted with Fred who reaches his limit in five minutes flat, and with his neighbour who can press on for half the afternoon. However, if we accept that the extremes must be dealt with on an individual basis, the very general guide of about fifteen to forty minutes may not be too far out.

On this assumption it is immediately apparent that more than one task must be provided for the hour period under discussion. Allowing for the time it will take to allocate tasks, to change from one to another and to clear up afterwards (especially with younger children), two or three tasks will be necessary over the age and ability range. The experienced teacher is not likely to have much difficulty in changing groups to new tasks at intervals appropriate to their probable span of concentration, but in the early stages of teaching this pattern of frequent change is not easy to handle. A compromise is therefore worth considering.

For this purpose, two main tasks, preferably divided by a short class activity, should be planned for all groups; but with two provisos:

(i) that any child who is really absorbed in the first one should be permitted to continue with it if he wishes to do so; and
(ii) that with top infants rather more than one hour may need to be timetabled in order that the two tasks can be effectively accomplished.

There should be a few 'secondary' occupations, known to the children and recognised as being available for their choice, if they finish early. There might be such things as:

(*a*) Working in the 'busy bay' (or something with a happier title if anyone is clever enough to think one up), where there are cards giving short assignments at different levels such as 'Trace this picture' and 'Write down all the things you can see beginning with *b*'.
(*b*) Reading in the 'quiet bay' (for pleasure, and not just to keep out of the way!).
(*c*) Using something from the 'odd-job shelf', where there is practical material such as envelopes containing words to be arranged in a sentence, word and sound matching dominoes, etc.
(*d*) Adding a bit more to some effort of personal interest, e.g. a book about insects, pictures of 'two' or of round things which are being collected and kept in a folder.

It should be understood by the children (albeit with some reminding) that if they finish early they should repair to one of these occupations until it is time for everybody to change to another task. It is not suggested that it all happens quite as smoothly in practice as the theory implies. Some children will still say 'What shall I do now?'; some will set off round the room trying hopefully to look busy but in fact doing nothing much at all; some will not even hope that they look busy. But if there is a choice of occupations which the children are supposed to undertake, the teacher can at least direct them to do so. Without this choice, she is forced to try and think of something each time for every child that finishes early, whereas if she organises the situation she may find that it makes fewer demands on her time and patience.

This plan is not effective with a reception class, or one in which the majority of children are very young. In this situation, at least three tasks and probably a short class activity must be arranged for an hour period, or there will be so many children finishing early that the system will break down. But once the majority of children are beyond this stage, two tasks for an hour work reasonably well. The number finishing early is not so large as to be unmanageable, and there is enough variety to take account of the child's need for change when his ability to concentrate on one task has come to an end.

3. Changeover from one activity to another

Having suggested that two main tasks should be planned for a period of approximately one hour (with 'secondary' tasks for early finishers and some modification for a reception class), it is wise to give some thought to the changeover from the first of these tasks to the second. This is the point at which confusion is likely to arise, especially with a large class, unless it is quite carefully planned.

At 'half-time', the position is that some children have finished early and (with encouragement) are now engaged upon their 'secondary' tasks; some were so nearly finished that a few minutes' warning has enabled them to make an extra effort and complete their assignment; some, and these characters are known to us all, are nowhere near finished despite constant prodding—but a further extension of time will not extract much more from them anyway; and a few are so absorbed that they wish to continue, and the teacher may well feel inclined to allow them to do so rather than insist upon their changing to the second task.

If the pattern is significantly different from this—if, for example, a very high proportion of the class regularly finishes early—it may be that the teacher is either overestimating the time required or underestimating the children's capacity. Some re-thinking of the tasks appropriate to the different groups might therefore be necessary.

However, it is never easy for the teacher, unless she is really very experienced, to direct all the groups from one task to another at more or less the same time without a fair amount of disruption while all this change and movement are taking place. It is very much easier to conduct the operation in three stages:

(i) Bring the first task to an end (except for the few who really wish to continue), and do any necessary clearing up.

(ii) Have a short class activity—possibly some number rhymes, or for older children a few minutes of 'I spy'—to settle them and gain their attention.

(iii) Allocate the next assignment to each group and set them on their way.

By this arrangement, it will be found that a period of one hour will, broadly speaking, allow twenty to twenty-five minutes for each task, plus the necessary time for starting them off and clearing up. The class activity between the two can be used as a sort of 'control mechanism' to vary the time given to the main tasks. For the children at the top of the infant school more than an hour may be necessary to carry out this plan, since many of them may have a longer effective span of concentration. And for the reception class, at least three tasks, similarly planned and divided, will be found advisable.

The teacher who knows her children will have a fairly good idea of how long they may reasonably be expected to remain on one assignment, and she will avoid rigidity by adapting any suggested design to the needs and circumstances of her own class. However, if she plans not only the assignments themselves but the changeover from one to another as well, she may find that this helps to make her lesson organisation run more smoothly.

4. Change of occupation and physical position

In planning the assignments to be given to the different groups, care must be taken to ensure that they give the children a change of occupation and also of physical position. An hour is not only too long for a young child to concentrate on one task; it is also too long for him to remain sitting in one position without becoming fidgety and restless, and fortunately this is something which organisation can help to avoid. One of the assignments should cause the child to move about in the room, and the other should require him to sit down, at least for much of the time. He may need to leave his chair temporarily to seek some information, but the assignment should, so to speak, be 'chair-based'. This implies very deliberate planning on the part of the teacher, but it is the kind of general plan which can be applied again and again so that the initial effort is fully justified in the long run. The detail of a plan of this nature will be suggested later.

5. Limitation of movement

In the organisation of the hour period under review, the teacher (and the children) will find it very much easier if not more than about half the class is on the move at the same time. This does not mean that movement has to be unnaturally restricted, or that the practical experience which all children need must be limited in some arbitrary way in order to satisfy organisational requirements. Children must have practical experience, and they indeed must move; but all thirty-five or forty of them do not have to be doing it at the same moment of time.

The use of a considerable variety of material and apparatus is involved in 3R work. This must be available in turn to all the children in the class, and it is necessary for the teacher to keep track of what they are all doing. She has to ensure that in the course of a day or a week every child has the opportunity to use the full range of material that is appropriate to him. Some of this material is more effectively handled from the child's chair. He cannot trace a picture or write a story or do a number jigsaw while he is moving about, and therefore one accepts that for part of the time he sits down anyway.

What is now being suggested is that this should be planned, and not left to chance. In this way, those who *must* move have more space and freedom to do so; and those who are sitting down are not being penalised, because they cannot conveniently do what they are doing in any other position. In an Integrated Day programme the situation is rather different, because children are doing other things besides 3Rs at any given time. They are therefore not likely to converge in such large numbers on the shop or the weighing table or the reading bay within a fairly short space of time. But in the kind of programme now under discussion this can very well happen if organisation does not prevent it, and then everyone's opportunities for constructive experience and movement may be much reduced.

6. Even use of room space

Following on from the last point, it is important that room space should be used evenly if there is to be maximum benefit from movement and from the use of practical materials. One can almost hear the teacher in a really small classroom sighing for room space to use in any kind of way at all, and for the luxury of having even half her children out of their seats and moving around in comfort. But on the other hand, even when one is fortunate enough to have space, this does not by itself provide the total solution. Once again it is organisation and planning which help to make the most of it.

The last two suggestions as well as this one are perhaps best illustrated by taking an example of how the two main 3R tasks could be planned. For this purpose, we will assume four groups: red, blue, green and yellow, with eight to ten children in each. The members of the group are not all at exactly the same stage, but they do fall within a recognisable band of attainment. For example, an assignment to the red group could be writing a 'story', and this might mean anything from constructing one original sentence to writing considerably more; but, as an assignment, it could apply to the whole group for the purpose of the teacher's planning. The children in the red group might sit at the 'red tables' if the teacher prefers it that way; or they might be scattered round all the tables. This is immaterial, so long as each child knows which group assignment applies to him.

For this particular 3R period, with a class for which two main tasks are appropriate, each group will be given a reading/writing assignment which is chair-based and a mathematics assignment which causes the children to move about in order to accomplish it. This meets the requirement that they must have a change of occupation and of physical position. In each half of the period two groups will have their reading/writing assignment and the other two will do their mathematics. In this way not more than about half the class will be on the move for any length of time.

It now remains for organisation to take account of the even use of room space. This might be achieved in the following way:

First main task

Red and blue groups	reading/writing assignments (perhaps writing a 'story')
Green group	measuring around the room

Yellow group	four children at water-play, the remainder shopping (this keeps the number at the shop small enough to avoid long queues)

Second main task

Red group	measuring around the room
Blue group	four on liquid measure (these children are past the 'water-play' stage), the remainder shopping
Green and yellow groups	reading / writing assignments (these might include 'dictating a story' to the teacher to be copied or traced, word and sentence matching, etc.)

The children who are engaged in shopping and water-play or liquid measure are, on the whole, using those areas of the room where the shop and the water are situated; so they are more or less out of each other's way. Those who are measuring therefore have more freedom of movement in the rest of the room. There will obviously be some overlap of areas as children move about to talk to one another or to the teacher, but generally speaking their assignments will base them in different parts of the classroom and it is less likely that there will be too great a concentration of children in any one place for long.

7. A written plan

When the teacher is very used to organising her class, and particularly when the framework of such an organisation is well established, her group plans will be second nature to her and she is not likely to have much difficulty in deciding what each is to do. However, until she reaches that stage she will find it well worth while to jot down these plans in note form in advance. Plans of this kind need to be very carefully thought out in the first place, and it is extremely difficult to do this effectively on the spur of the moment. Advance planning can do so much to give the teacher confidence and to help her organisation to run smoothly that she will surely feel the time spent on it to be justified. In addition it will help her to make sure that all the children are undertaking, in turn, all the 3R activities which are part of the total programme of her class.

8. Allocation of assignments to groups

When a teacher has to allocate assignments to a number of different groups, it is sometimes very difficult for her not to keep the last group waiting so long that its members become rather restive and noisy in the interval. With young children, 'so long' may mean only a few minutes, but that is quite long enough to generate a fair amount of restlessness.

A little planning can do something to help this situation. It is quite often possible to estimate which assignment is going to require the longest explanation. This group should be left until last, but the children in it should be given a temporary 'task' to keep them busy until the teacher is free. Indeed the teacher's plan should take this into account, and should quite deliberately avoid more than one assignment which will take much time to introduce.

This applies particularly when the 'assignment' for one group, or part of a group, consists of some direct teaching of the next stage of a particular process, which the teacher has planned for that day (for there is no doubt that, however 'indirect' modern methods may seem to be, direct teaching of an individual or a group *must* take place if real progress is to be made).

The matter of the allocation of assignments to groups is perhaps more obvious than some other aspects of organisation. Yet it involves something which can help to eliminate a potential source of minor disturbance and it may therefore be worth noting when the teacher is considering her detailed plans.

9. Introduction of new apparatus

This is really a corollary of the point just made, but it is easy to overlook it when plans are being formulated. When new apparatus is introduced, some explanation will almost certainly be necessary to the children who are to use it. Because it is unfamiliar, even quite advanced children may need to discuss it with the teacher if they are to use it to advantage, and younger or slower children will nearly always need some additional help until they feel quite at home with it.

New apparatus, therefore, should never be introduced to more than one group at a time. The others should be given assignments with which they are already familiar, so that the teacher can concentrate a little more attention on the group with the new material. They may well need to use it more than once before it is comfortably familiar to them; but it will be of greater benefit if the teacher recognises this and restricts her new apparatus to the one group until she is satisfied that they can deal with it easily enough for her to discontinue the extra help.

10. The teacher's attention

The last of these considerations concerns a problem which experience overcomes. However, it is one which the teacher who is just beginning often finds very difficult to take in her stride, important though it is in terms of class management.

She has to aim, right from the start, at being able to direct her attention to one group, while at the same time spreading it over the whole class so that the children are aware all the time that she knows what they are doing. At first it seems almost impossible simultaneously to give that additional help to one group, to discuss for a moment John's 'tall tower' on the other side of the room, to write 'hippopotamus' in Sally's word-book and to stop Barry, who is round the corner, from stuffing paper towels into the milk bottle when he is supposed to be 'having experience of water-play'. The temptation is to attend almost exclusively to the group which is doing something new and to 'switch off' the rest of the class. It is astonishing how quickly children become aware of this situation, and before she knows where she is the unhappy teacher finds that riot and civil commotion have broken out all round her.

There is no plain and simple solution to this, but it is helped by good planning and organisation. The suggestions already made—such as the calculated avoidance of more than one assignment requiring extra attention, 'chair-based' or 'area-based' tasks for certain children, the reassurance of knowing beforehand what each group is to do and the note of confidence which this gives to the teacher's voice—all help to create the kind of atmosphere in which the children recognise that the teacher knows what is happening. Having worked towards this atmosphere, the teacher must be very firm with herself, and be always conscious of the need to look around frequently; to move over to another group or to one child for a minute or two before returning to the scene of concentrated effort; and generally to make her presence felt in all parts of the room, so that it almost seems as though she really has eyes in the back of her head. This is indeed not easy to begin with, but it is not impossible. The teacher may take comfort in the knowledge that this is a fairly temporary problem and that it does become easier with experience; and if she is aware of the necessity to train herself in this way she is half way to success. This kind of self-training is essential if group and individual teaching are to work well, and the teacher has everything to gain from acknowledging its importance and coming to terms with it as soon as she can.

THE RECEPTION CLASS

It might be helpful to conclude this chapter with a few comments about the specific problems of organising a reception class. Although in all small schools, and in larger ones where a different form of organisation is in operation (e.g. family or parallel grouping), the reception class, as such, does not exist, it is still quite widely found where preference or particular circumstances seem to make its retention desirable.

One of the main problems encountered by the teacher of a reception class is that so many of her children are very unskilled in the ways which help her to organise. There is so little that they can do without a good deal of her help, and because they are so young and school is unfamiliar they have a need for more of her attention anyway. A further problem is that there will be some children who are as advanced as many who are not in the reception class, and if they are not stretched they will be bored and unhappy; and there will be others who are really still at the nursery stage and for whom 'real' school and being away from home all day is a pretty traumatic experience. Somehow the teacher has to unite these extremes into a coherent class which can be organised so that the strongly individual needs of the children can be satisfied.

Once again, it would be idle to pretend that there is an easy solution in these circumstances. Although a reception class can be quite remarkably rewarding, the sheer professional skill required to organise and teach it may well be greater than is needed for any other age group throughout school. However, there are certain aspects of organisation which can help to smooth over some of the difficulties attendant upon the first weeks in school of a large number of children. Some attempt should be made to indicate what these are and to suggest a constructive line of approach.

1. 'Assignments' (it seems such a grand word to use in this context) should be broken down, to begin with, into small units of not more than ten or fifteen minutes each. At first, most of the children are likely to be doing very similar things, since the teacher cannot have an accurate idea of what they can do in order to group them. For the majority of children, grouping in anything but a very loose form is unlikely to emerge much before half term, but this does not preclude the use of the kind of assignments appropriate at this stage. However, more definite grouping is possible almost from the beginning with the children who are fairly plainly at either extreme of the attainment range.

Those who, for one reason or another, seem unable to settle to anything at all, even for a few minutes, are an inevitable part of the reception class scene. The teacher must do whatever she can with them, offering them alternative occupations in quick succession until she hits upon something which will hold their attention for a little longer. She may need to take a particularly tearful or unsettled child by the hand and allow him to walk round with her while she sees to the others, and sometimes she can find 'jobs' for one or two to do until she has time to attend more closely to them. However, a frequent change of occupation (and physical position) is very necessary for most children in the early stages of the reception class, and organisation must take this into account.

2. The assignments should be interspersed with a variety of class activities to encourage cohesion and a sense of 'belonging'. They might take the form of nursery rhymes, songs, movement poems and finger plays, number jingles, short class discussions and stories. These class activities should not last long, but they will help to give all the children a feeling of having the teacher's attention, with the sense of security that this brings.

3. Any instructions to the class should be separated into small components and sometimes physically assisted or demonstrated; and they should be applied to a group at a time if possible rather than to the whole class. For example, a request to 'make a line ready to go to assembly' is likely to be almost totally unproductive. The children may, if the teacher is fortunate, move in the general direction of the door. But the 'line' will be an amorphous mass of little bodies trying hopefully to get into some vague sort of order, and a certain amount of pushing and shoving by the more intrepid characters will not add much to the shape of the required line.

It will be a good deal more successful if the teacher stands by the door and calls two children to start the line. She can then summon the remainder, preferably a few at a time, and help them into a sufficiently manageable formation to take them along to the hall. If the class is small it is more natural to take them with her in a group and not worry about a line at all. But if numbers are large this is not very practicable, and she must help the children to make a line, table by table, until they have done it often enough to be able to manage it comfortably themselves. This 'breaking down' of instructions into small components helps the organisation of a reception class very considerably.

4. It is much less difficult to organise older children, when there are a good many things they can do themselves without the teacher's constant help. With a reception class this is not nearly as easy, but it is possible. There are things which even very young children can do, if not quite by themselves at least with the minimum of supervision. They can use some of the practical equipment in the room, e.g. the sand and water, the balances, the number jigsaws, etc. (accepting that the teacher

must help them to begin with and 'visit' them from time to time to discuss what they are doing). They can draw and trace, activities which are valuable for learning pencil control and the beginning of writing. They can play lotto games, for word and number matching. They can be introduced before long to some of the very simple card apparatus, and once they are familiar with it they can use it without a great deal of help.

Any of these activities, if planned and organised carefully beforehand, will keep most reception class children profitably occupied for perhaps ten minutes or a quarter of an hour, without needing attention the whole of the time. However, this will happen only if the teacher consciously trains the children to use these materials without constant reference to her and if she insists that they do so as soon as she reasonably can. Certainly she will find the organisation of a reception class difficult unless she succeeds in training most of the children in this way fairly quickly. Gradually their capacity for independent application will extend, and the teacher's plans can be adjusted to take advantage of this in order to introduce more individual and group assignments. And as the children become more familiar with the organisational framework of the class, their greater sense of security will help them to be a little more self-reliant and to share more readily the teacher's time with the others in the class.

5. The fact that so many children in a reception class are, in some ways, comparatively unskilled makes it only too easy for those who are really quite advanced to be insufficiently stretched. They will probably emerge very soon as a recognisable group, and it is most important that the level of their activity should match the effort of which they are capable. This is very much a matter of organisation and planning: of taking account of what these children can do and of making sure that appropriate experience and materials are made available to them. The children who are the least advanced must also have special provision from an early stage, but in a reception class their needs are generally less likely to be overlooked.

The organisation of a full reception class undoubtedly

presents its problems and there is little to be gained by underestimating them. The teacher's success will depend largely upon her skill in handling these very young children and on her ability to give them a sense of community and security while encouraging the development of every child. However, it is a mistake to believe that because their skills are limited it is not possible to plan and organise the daily programme of reception class children. Their very lack of skill makes organisation even more imperative, and there can be little doubt that the teacher who gives them a well-defined structure in which to develop their skills will be adding much to the value and enjoyment of their early experience of school.

Chapter 5

Integration or Disintegration

The kind of fairly traditional daily programme discussed in the last chapter is based on the principle that the teacher, within certain general limits, decides what the children are to do. In any programme the teacher ultimately makes this decision, but in the traditional pattern her choice is more apparent and direct and the children are accustomed to accepting this. The timetable may well be very fluid and it will certainly be flexible enough to respect the children's interests and their own personal needs. However, the element of teacher-direction is unmistakable and the children expect their teacher to give them an immediate lead in many of their activities.

This does not in any way suggest that some very good teaching does not take place in such a system, and it is widely and successfully used. However, an alternative to the time-honoured teacher-direction has for some time been steadily developed, and is now found almost exclusively in many areas. This alternative has come to be known generally as the 'Integrated Day'.

The Integrated Day is, essentially, a form of organisation in which the *child* exercises a greater degree of choice about what he is going to do and when he is going to do it, and the teacher integrates his daily programme so that learning and progress take place. It can be outstandingly successful; and it can be dismally bad. Some attempt should be made to analyse the reasons for these two extremes.

At its best, and in circumstances for which it is suitable, the Integrated Day offers a form of organisation which has solid advantages and can lead to undeniably good results. It makes possible for the teacher an individual approach which enables her to take greater account of each child's interests and his rate of progress. She can cater more easily for differences in the speed at which children work and in the length of time for which they can effectively concentrate. She can take advantage of the fact that most people work to more purpose and with greater enjoyment at something which they have chosen to do. By allowing the child to choose his activity (within reason) the teacher may encourage him to develop his initiative and his sense of responsibility, and she can often make use of momentum and enthusiasm which may have evaporated a little later.

From the teacher's point of view, the immense advantage is that she does seem to have more time to attend to individual children. It is not easy to put one's finger on just why this is so, but it may well be the effect of an accumulation of many odd minutes saved and of a reduction in her 'administrative' duties (such as allocating group assignments). When an Integrated Day organisation is working really well, the children do use their initiative to help themselves and to act independently. It is, of course, possible for this to happen with a really well-managed traditional programme. But it happens to a greater extent with the Integrated Day, because the very nature of the system develops to the full just those capacities in children which help to free the teacher from a multitude of time-consuming duties.

However, the very fact that an Integrated Day can be so successful makes it all the more important that its difficulties and demands should be honestly recognised. It is unfortunately a fact that when it does not work the results can be almost totally unprofitable for the children, and demoralising and exhausting for the teacher. It is probably no exaggeration to say that with a more formal structure somebody is almost certain to learn something on the way, whereas with a disorganised Integrated Day it is perfectly possible for no child to make any real progress at all except that which comes about more or less by accident.

It is only by carefully examining the organisation of an Integrated Day, by considering its aims, by anticipating its particular problems and by quite deliberately seeking to build a structure which is sound enough to be of real educational value that one can answer the critics who know only of its ill effects. One should not have to be defensive about a form of organisation which has long since proved its worth, but too often one is. And the best way of overcoming this is to try to consider the question critically and dispassionately, and to avoid some of the pitfalls by being aware of what they are.

The aims of an Integrated Day are material to its structure; and one must assume that these aims cannot be achieved as effectively with a more formal organisation, or there would be little point in changing to an Integrated Day at all. We are not here concerned with broad philosophical aims, but with the practical objectives of good class organisation which have already been summarised: the happiness and well-being of every child and his progress according to his capacity; the encouragement of initiative and self-reliance in an atmosphere of controlled freedom; and the individual approach in teaching that good modern practice requires. The supporters of the Integrated Day believe that these objectives are more readily attained if both children and teacher are free to follow a less centrally directed programme, or, more accurately, a programme in which central direction is less evident. *But it is this last qualification which is at the heart of the divergence between theory and really successful practice.*

For it is a fallacy to believe that a well integrated programme, in which the child exercises a fairly considerable degree of choice and responsibility for what he does, requires no structuring by the teacher at all. The reality is, in fact, just the reverse. The teacher's planning and organisation are certainly unobtrusive, and the children are much less aware that there is direction in their choice. However, the structuring behind the scenes of a successfully integrated programme is often very extensive indeed. It has to be even more methodical and even more carefully planned than is necessary when there is a fairly obvious framework of organisation on which to depend. There is no doubt whatever that if the teacher does not have a clear idea of what her children should do, then certainly they will have no idea at all; and this is the point at which things begin to go wrong.

Unfortunately it is sometimes believed that the only thing necessary for the successful introduction of an Integrated Day is that a decision should be made to that effect and all will thereafter be well. Perhaps this is an over-simplification, but in practice it is not always far from the truth. Admittedly the decision must be made; but this is only the beginning. An immense amount of thought and care must go into planning the kind of organisation that such a programme will require, and above all into introducing it gradually so that neither teacher nor children will find themselves lost on the way.

It must be conceded that agreement on this point is not universal. The purists argue that an Integrated Day organisation is not worthy of the name unless and until the entire programme is fully integrated and the child's freedom of choice is complete. However, one is not obliged to accept these two assumptions, and indeed one may wholly reject them. There is no reason at all to suppose that there is just one definable pattern which has title to the name 'Integrated Day', while no other pattern has the right to any such title. There is no blueprint or set of rules which must be slavishly followed. It would be unacceptable if there were, for no part of education is a package. There is, and there should be, variety of form and of degree, which in some circumstances may mean more integration and in others less. There is force and wisdom in taking into account the many variables which apply in schools: the area, the background and experience of the children, the possibilities of the classroom, the personality and the strength of the teacher and her own teaching techniques.

It is a disservice to the benefits of the Integrated Day to set it apart in inverted commas, to make it an end in itself in the name of 'progressive education'. This is to diminish it, to make a 'band wagon' of it instead of according to it the value of being a natural and sensible development in circumstances where it is likely to be educationally sound.

The circumstances in which it may be of very limited value—indeed, where it may be of much less value than a traditional teacher-directed programme—are primarily those in which for one reason or another the children are particularly insecure. This may be because of a high proportion of difficult home backgrounds, or because of large-scale population movement in a new area where the children have not yet had time to settle down, or because of exceptional strains and severe disciplinary problems. In conditions such as these children badly need the security of clear teacher-direction and of an easily recognised organisation with which they can quickly become familiar. They are just not in a position to be able to accept too quickly the responsibility of making decisions about what they will do.

In due course, the first gentle moves towards integration, planned so that the children do not feel any loss of support, may well be good for them. If the change is made in small, easily accepted steps it may ultimately be possible for them to enjoy the advantages of a good deal of integration in those areas of the programme in which it would be most beneficial. In other words, these children can have the kind of Integrated Day which is suitable for them in their particular circumstances; and if it is not fully integrated at an early stage—or at all—who is to say that this does not justify the use of the term?

Integration is integration, whether in whole or in part; and partial integration which works, and which in time is worth taking further, is incomparably superior and more worthy of recognition than total integration which does not, in educational terms, really get off the ground. Total integration can be most hearteningly effective, but where this is true it will remarkably often be found that much care and thought accompanied its gradual development, and that it operates in circumstances which are favourable to its success.

An important factor contributing to the quality of an Integrated Day is the ability of the teacher to keep control of her class and to retain the confidence of her children while the change is being made. At first sight, words like 'control' and 'discipline' do not seem to fit very well into a form of organisation which is partly justified by its advantages in developing the child's sense of responsibility and his capacity to act independently. However, it is these very advantages which need a controlled atmosphere if they are to flourish. Young children cannot act responsibly if they do not have an orderly environment in which to do so, because few things make them less likely to restrain themselves than a situation in which restraint is not generally exercised.

It is again a matter of their sense of security. If this is threatened, they will react in the only way open to them. The quiet and timorous children will become even more withdrawn, and they may suffer quite severely; the boisterous characters will become even more boisterous; and those who fall into neither category will be bored or confused or both. They will behave according to the demands of the moment, and they will contract out of individual or concerted effort because it is beyond them to do anything else.

At all costs, the teacher must prevent this from happening. She must make certain that there is sufficient order and control in her class to show the children what is expected of them and to define the limits of their independence quite clearly. As with her organisation in an Integrated Day, her discipline must of necessity be less obtrusive and direct or the children's sense of independence will disappear. Yet this makes it more difficult for her. It is perfectly possible to keep young children under powerful restraint while they are in the classroom if this is the object of the exercise, but the infant teacher rightly discards the possibility. Neither is it excessively difficult, with good organisation, to keep the reins in one's hands when there is movement and discussion, but with a strong element of teacher-direction. However, in an Integrated Day, where this direction is so much less evident, the teacher's control must be of a very high order if children are to have the freedom to choose their activities and to behave responsibly while exercising this freedom. It is very much more a matter of atmosphere than of an authority constantly imposed.

This is demanding of the teacher, but when she is successful it brings its rewards and she is much more likely to be successful if she does not try to move too fast. It can be disastrous to sweep away a familiar pattern and try to replace it one Monday morning with something which is fundamentally different. It is asking for trouble to impose upon children the responsibility of choice without first preparing and training them to accept it. It is also asking too much of a teacher, particularly if she has no experience of the organisation of an Integrated Day, to adjust her sights and modify her programme so radically, and to keep control of a situation in which thirty or forty children are too quickly thrown upon their own resources. It is no wonder that in these circumstances they can run wild and engage in aimless and time-wasting activities which even the most charitable have difficulty in describing as 'educational'. The children suffer from being put in this position; the teacher loses confidence and becomes frustrated and tired; and before long the Integrated Day is thoroughly, and unjustly, discredited.

This may be a black picture, but it is not altogether imaginary; and it can be avoided. There is little to lose and everything to gain from moving slowly and laying solid foundations on which to build. Success will come far more quickly in the end, and the transition will have been a happy one instead of a painful and punishing experience. When the transition has been completed, the critics may be invited to judge the results.

Chapter 6

The Transition from a Traditional Programme to an Integrated Day

One has to accept that if a teacher without previous experience of an Integrated Day is appointed to a school where it is already well established, she must adapt to this form of organisation from the beginning. Though children should not be subjected to this kind of immediate change, it is not always avoidable for a teacher; and some suggestions which may help her in this situation are included in the next chapter. However, we are now concerned with the circumstances of reorganising a class to allow for a gradual transition from a traditional programme to a partially or a fully Integrated Day.

It should be said at once that most of the suggestions which follow are not intended to represent the one and only way of undertaking the exercise. It is true that certain essentials will be emphasised, particularly with regard to the early training of children which is fundamental to the subsequent organisation of an integrated programme. However, once the foundations have been laid, the detail of the later stages may well be varied. A teacher who is considering making the transition will extract from any proposals those which she feels may succeed in her classroom; she will add ideas of her own; and she will reject suggestions which seem to her of doubtful value. It is on this assumption that a concrete plan is put forward. It is not a 'blueprint', and it does not exclude workable alternatives. But its proposals are unambiguous, or it would not have a case to present.

The extent to which it is advisable to integrate the children's programme and the length of time which the transition should take are dependent upon circumstances. For this reason, a step-by-step approach has much in its favour. The children can be trained to accept each step, and as each is established and is running smoothly another advance can be made. If further advance is thought to be unwise because of particular conditions, the position can be left as it is and any further modification deferred until the time is favourable. On the other hand, if circumstances are such that a more rapid transition promises to be successful the rate of change can be accelerated. The flexibility of this approach is perhaps one of its advantages.

It is difficult to make a realistic assessment of how long the transitional period should be, because any generalised statement is open to so many qualifications. However, some kind of estimation might be useful, if only as a rough-and-ready guide. With older children in the infant school, in circumstances which are likely to be favourable to reorganisation, the transition to a partially integrated programme might be accomplished in a term. If the junior school to which they will transfer at the end of the year is organised on traditional lines it might be as well to attempt no further integration in order to avoid exposing the children to too much change of pattern. If, on the other hand, this reservation does not apply, total integration may be complete by the end of the second term.

In a family-grouped class containing the full age range, either the change would have to be a good deal slower because the younger children would need more support in adapting to it, or the teacher would have to integrate part of her class more rapidly than the rest. This is not as difficult as it sounds, as will emerge from the detailed stages suggested later in this chapter.

If, however, a change to an Integrated Day is being considered for a reception class, or one in which there is a high proportion of very young children, the transition must take considerably longer. In fact, the first term will be entirely a preparatory period and integration, as such, will not be evident at all. In the second term the top groups may begin to accept comfortably the responsibility of choice, and by the end of the year quite a marked degree of integration may well be achieved.

On the other hand, if conditions are unfavourable to

extensive change the whole operation could take a great deal longer and be limited in its scope. The criterion should never be 'How *quickly* can we integrate?'. The only criterion that matters is 'How *well* can we integrate?'. The school which in difficult conditions has, in two or three years, achieved partial integration which is really successful is educationally on solid ground. The school which, however, claims more, but in which organisational problems are still discouragingly apparent, has achieved much less that can in all honesty be commended.

When we have considered the time which the transition from a traditionally organised programme could take, our next concern is with the stages by which integration might be effected. The duration of each stage will vary according to conditions, and the question of whether or not all the stages are completed will depend upon the issues which have already been discussed. However, it is fairly safe to say that where there is doubt about the wisdom of moving to the next stage, it is better to wait a little longer. Delay is less likely to bring difficulties than too precipitate an advance.

SUGGESTED STAGES

Stage I

This stage is essentially one of preparation and training, with integration as its ultimate objective. In a well organised class it will not last long, unless the children are very young or there are exceptional circumstances which justify a cautious pace. It is, however, the stage during which the foundations of successful integration are laid, and for this reason it should not be unduly hurried. Time spent on adequate preparation will pay dividends when subsequent stages are reached.

Basically, there are three important areas to which training for the introduction of an integrated programme should be especially directed:

1. Grouping the children.
2. Training them in the use of materials and in class organisation.
3. Establishing discipline and control.

1. Grouping

This was discussed at length in Chapter 4 in connection with the organisation of a traditional programme. It is included here because a grouping pattern is often considered to be unnecessary with integration. However, grouping has two unmistakable advantages. The first is that the introduction of an Integrated Day is very much easier if the children are organised in identifiable groups. The second is that even when the programme is eventually fully integrated, grouping can assist organisation in many important ways. It is true that by then the children will not often work in groups, because learning and teaching will be very much on an individual basis. The group as an organisational unit will, however, still have a place, and this is a good reason for establishing it securely at the beginning. Its function in a fully integrated programme will be apparent when the management of such a programme is later examined.

2. Training the children in the use of materials and in class organisation

All that has been said about the introduction of new material, about training the children to use it without constant reference to the teacher, about their collecting it themselves where possible and putting it away—these and most of the other details of class organisation which were considered earlier apply also to the introduction of an Integrated Day, but with an added proviso: they apply even more emphatically than they do when the class is organised on more traditional lines. For the fact is that when integration really takes place, and the children are engaged in all manner of different activities, it is quite impossible for the teacher to fetch and carry for them and to deal with every detail that upwards of thirty children feel disposed to refer to her.

The success of an Integrated Day will stand or fall by the children's ability to act independently, to make decisions and to help themselves. Teacher-direction in its obvious form cannot recede into the background until the children have been trained to fill the gap which it appears to leave. Good training and preparation in this respect are therefore essential if there is to be a strong foundation on which to build an integrated structure. In other words, organisation within a traditional programme must be really sound and the children must be quite familiar with what is expected of them before the first step towards integration is taken. If not, it will be like asking them 'to run before they can walk'. Their responsibility for what they do cannot successfully be extended until they can comfortably accept that which a good traditional organisation requires of them. Training them in this really vital area must therefore come first.

3. Establishing discipline and control

Reference has already been made to the demands which the children's independence of action implicit in an Integrated Day makes upon the teacher's ability to control them. The necessity for this is restated here because ineffective control may well defeat the finest organisation and the most carefully laid plans. 'Controlled freedom', in which each child can satisfy his own needs without thereby preventing others from doing the same, is important enough to delay any move towards integration until the teacher is confident that she can handle the class without undue strain. When she knows that she can allow freedom without licence, and variety of purpose without confusion, she is safe in assuming that she can extend the children's responsibility without fear of the consequences. She must not, however, underestimate the importance of achieving this objective before embarking upon the next stage of the transition.

Summarising the first stage, it could be said that by the end of it the children should be used to:

(*a*) Working in groups, and individually, in a constructive and sensible way.
(*b*) Organising themselves, within reason, in collecting their own materials, working with them and putting them away when they have finished.
(*c*) Accepting the teacher's authority in an atmosphere of 'controlled freedom', and recognising that some measure of self-discipline is necessary in the interests of others.
(*d*) Acknowledging the principle of moving from one task to another without intermediate reference to the teacher.

With these foundations firmly laid, there is every justification for anticipating the next stage with confidence in its success.

Stage II

It is at this stage that integration begins, but only on a very limited scale. The teacher now sets aside a period of time each day—say one hour, or less if the children are rather young—for which she allocates to each group two specific tasks. In order to show how a traditional lesson plan can be adapted quite naturally to introduce an integrated programme, we will refer to the examples used in the proposals for the hour period of 3R work suggested in Chapter 4.
These were:

Red group	(i)	writing a 'story'
	(ii)	'measuring around the room'
Blue group	(i)	writing a 'story'
	(ii)	four on liquid measure, the remainder shopping
Green group	(i)	'measuring around the room'
	(ii)	a reading/writing assignment, possibly 'dictating' to the teacher a sentence to be traced or copied
Yellow group	(i)	four on water-play, the remainder shopping
	(ii)	a reading/writing assignment, possibly word and sentence matching.

In each case the reading/writing assignment was chair-based and the mathematics assignment gave opportunity for movement. Supplementary tasks were provided for early finishers, and the two parts of the lesson were divided by a class activity.

The same basic plan is applicable to the limited integration now proposed for this stage, but some adaptation is necessary to allow for certain essential differences in the two forms of organisation. In the traditional pattern, the teacher not only allocated the tasks to the groups—she also determined the order in which they were to be undertaken. She could therefore directly control the amount of movement in the room and the areas in which it would take place. She now specifies the two tasks which she wants each group to aim at completing during the hour, but she allows each child to decide the order in which he will do them.

This modification has the following organisational consequences:

1. There is no longer any need to split the blue and yellow groups for their water and shopping activities. This was necessary in the traditional plan, because the teacher had to avoid directing a full group to an activity which could not comfortably accommodate so many children simultaneously.

Now, however, all the children in one of these groups can be given shopping as their mathematics assignment, on the assumption that some will choose to do this as their first task and some as their second. Furthermore, until they are used to a considerable measure of integration, they will find it easier if those who shop together are at a roughly comparable level of attainment. At a later stage, children of widely differing ability will work sensibly and profitably at the same activity; but it is better to make the change more gradually from the familiar pattern of working together in the groups which they know.

Assuming eight to ten children in each group, there might be some slight difficulty in assigning water-play to a whole group. Five could be just too many to use the water-trough at the same time, and in this case the group could be offered the additional alternative of weighing. This is a matter of detail which the teacher would need to decide at the time.

2. In the plan for the traditional programme, the green group was to 'measure around the room' in the first part of the period, followed by the red group in the second part. This was the one activity which permitted movement all over the room space, and the plan limited the number that could be engaged on it at any one time to a maximum of about ten.

Because of the amount of movement involved in this particular activity, it would probably be wise in the new plan to restrict it to one group only. It is more difficult to ensure that a voluntary limitation of numbers is being observed when the children are all over the classroom than when they are based in one area, as in shopping or water-play; and the risk of too many choosing this activity at one time is rather too great.

The red group's mathematics assignment might therefore be altered to measuring from work cards. However, since this activity is chair-based, their reading/writing assignment must also be changed in order to give them enough movement. Instead of writing a story on this occasion, they might use practical word-building and phonic apparatus. This could include dominoes, 'Lexicon' and other games, which would give the children enough movement and change of physical position to compensate for the chair-based mathematics; and the activity might conveniently take place on the floor in the home bay or some other area with a reasonable amount of space, in order to keep the red group more or less out of the way of the children engaged in measuring. It is this kind of modification which helps to reduce the risk of undue disturbance in the early stages of introducing an integrated programme.

3. The class activity which divided the two main parts of the lesson in the earlier pattern will no longer be required. The children will now move to the second task as they complete the first, and they will not all do this at the same time because of differences in the speed at which they work. There is therefore much less likelihood of confusion than when the whole class is changing over at the same time—and it was to avoid this that the class activity was originally suggested.

The teacher can now allocate the two main tasks to each group at the beginning of the period, together with one supplementary task for those who complete both assignments early. Organisation is thus simplified, because there is only one occasion instead of two when supplementary tasks may be needed to fill a possible gap. There is no reason why there should not be a short class activity at the end of the hour, if the teacher feels this would help to avoid a ragged conclusion until the new organisation is familiar and firmly established.

As far as the children are concerned, the new pattern brings other changes to which they must accommodate. It delegates to them three important areas of responsibility:

(i) That of putting into practice the principle of completing one task and beginning another without necessarily referring to the teacher for direction at the point of change.
(ii) That of exercising a degree of choice and of organising their time so that the two tasks are accomplished in a given period.
(iii) That of arranging their programme to take account of the need for the number engaged on certain activities to be limited.

To a child this extension of responsibility is significant; and the advantage of a carefully phased plan which introduces integration gradually is that it enables the children to become accustomed to responsibility on a small scale before they are asked to accept it over a wider field.

These areas of responsibility must, at this stage, be very clearly defined. For example, the teacher must tell the children (and probably keep telling them for a while) that there must not be more than four at the water-trough at one time, or six at the shop or five in the reading corner. Given the training and preparation which they have had in Stage I, it is not too difficult for them to accept the responsibility of changing the order of their choice if necessary in the interests of others. This is where the atmosphere of 'controlled freedom' which the children have been trained to respect is shown to be an essential element in class organisation. If one of Christopher's tasks is shopping, and he finds six already at the shop by the time he gets there, he must agree that he has then to 'choose' his other assignment as his first task.

This leads to two observations. The first is that under the new plan it is numerically possible for eight or ten children to choose to shop at the same time. If it should happen that they have chosen this as their first task there is no particular problem, because the last children to make the decision must fall back upon their other task and accept that this restriction is necessary. If, however, they have all completed one task and shopping is the only choice that remains open to them, the teacher must intervene in order to resolve the difficulty. She must offer an alternative task to those children who now cannot shop, and adjust her plans to give them shopping experience on another occasion.

This situation does not, of course, often arise. It can come about only in a particular combination of circumstances, which by the law of averages is unlikely to be frequent. However, it can happen. The teacher must acknowledge the possibility and be ready to deal with it, or there will be a weak link in her organisation which might let her down. One weak link will not cause the whole structure to topple; but links are cumulatively important, and it is always in the teacher's interest to anticipate weaknesses and to eliminate them before they can reach damaging proportions.

The second observation is that the restriction of Christopher's choice to only one of his two tasks is, in fact, to deprive him of choice altogether—and choice is one of the stated benefits of integration. However, this restriction imposed upon Christopher is temporary, and it is of value to his developing sense of responsibility that he should accept temporary restrictions when it is evident that these are necessary. Later on, when he has more than two tasks from which to choose, his freedom in this particular respect will be less limited. But by then he will be carrying other responsibilities, which will be less onerous if he has already grown accustomed to them from his earlier experience.

This stage of the transition from a traditional programme introduces only a small measure of integration. Yet it is a large enough step for many children to take with confidence, and for the teacher to handle easily unless she is very experienced at organising an Integrated Day. And it does achieve some important intermediate objectives on the way to further advance, both organisationally and in terms of the children's experience of a new way of working.

Until this stage of the transition has been confidently absorbed, there seems little to be gained from trying to take reorganisation any further. Indeed, in very difficult conditions it may not be advisable to go much beyond this at all, except over a long period of time. However, this does not invalidate the benefits of even limited integration, and in all but the most unfavourable circumstances the next step can be taken without causing undue difficulty either to the teacher or to her class.

Stage III

This is a development of Stage II, and again the keynote is gradual advance. The teacher now takes reorganisation a little further, by extending the period of integration in length and by increasing the number of tasks to be accomplished. It is an advantage to begin with the top group and include the rest of the class by degrees, since the more able children will have less difficulty in organising their time over a longer period and in supporting the responsibility of more choice. The less advanced children may well need to move more slowly, and they will benefit from some extra help and attention in assisting them to make the change.

Bearing this in mind, the first step would be to lengthen the red group's period of integration from an hour to an hour and a half, and to add a third assignment to their two 3R tasks. This should be a practical or creative activity—perhaps to do something more to the model village. The time given over to these assignments might now be 11 a.m. to noon, and 1.30 p.m. to 2 p.m., since it is very necessary for children to become accustomed to the idea of organising their time across a break in school hours. The children in the red group may undertake their three assignments in order of their own preference, but they must try to complete them all in the time allowed unless there is a very good reason for their being unable to do so.

The blue, green and yellow groups will at first continue with their programme as before, i.e. the two 3R activities for the morning period. From 1.30 p.m. to 2 p.m., when the red group is still occupied with its assignments, these three groups can begin their normal 'free' or 'creative' activity period; and the children from the red group may join them as they complete the third of their tasks. The programme for the rest of the day would follow the usual routine.

As the teacher judges that the blue group is ready for a

more extended period of integrated work, she will arrange for those children a programme comparable to that of the red group; and she will in due course follow a similar pattern with the remaining two groups.

The extension of integrated activity to one group at a time is, in practice, not difficult to organise. It must, certainly, be carefully planned, but so must all effective organisation. There is, however, one potential problem which the teacher may avoid if she is prepared for it. It can arise if the groups which have two assignments merge with those that have three. This presents the child who is unwilling to apply himself with a first-rate opportunity for doing nothing very constructive if the teacher is not watchful of the possibility. Bobby can sound very convincing when he says that the paper aeroplanes he is trying out are being developed for the airport extension he is planning for the model village. This could at some other time be a legitimate activity; but when it transpires that he is not in the group concerned just then with the model village, and that he should in fact be either shopping or writing a story, his motives are open to more than a little doubt. His own assignments can be sadly neglected if he professes to attach himself too frequently to the fringes of another group's activity.

By the end of Stage III, most of the children are becoming very used to having a choice of tasks and making their own decisions about the order in which they will do them. They are also (Bobby excepted) more skilled at planning their time so as to complete, or be within sight of completing, their assignments. It is not yet too difficult for the teacher to keep track of what the children in the various groups are accomplishing, and to apply an occasional judicious prod when this seems necessary. She should not feel that she must be too rigid about insisting that every child completes all his tasks. She should aim at a balance between cutting short genuine effort and interest, and allowing children to take unnecessarily long over one task at the expense of others. However, deliberate training is necessary here for some children, or a further extension of their choice could be ineffective. All children will not invariably do everything they are supposed to do just because the teacher has a plan; but they are rather more likely to make the effort if they know that she is aware of what they should be doing, and that she expects them to reach the goal she has set if they possibly can.

There is one remaining point which is perhaps worth noting. The teacher should ensure that whenever necessary one of the 'assignments' of a group (or part of a group) takes the form of some direct teaching, to enable those children to progress to the next stage of their learning. This, of course, reduces the group's choice of tasks on that day, but this will not hurt the children or violate any principles of integration. Plans must allow for direct teaching in the same way as they allow for any other activity, and this becomes particularly important as the period of integrated work is lengthened. There is nothing about an Integrated Day which makes direct teaching any less essential than it has always been in a programme organised on traditional lines.

Stage IV

Until now, there has been much more teacher-direction in the children's activities than is normally found in an Integrated Day. In Stage IV it begins to be withdrawn, so that it is less evident to the children and their own independence of choice and action seems to them to be more complete. This means organising the class so that the child, within the limits of an overall plan, knows which tasks to do, instead of the teacher having to tell him. It also means lengthening the periods of integrated activity and increasing the child's personal responsibility for arranging his programme. Provided the earlier stages have prepared him adequately to take this step, and accepting that teacher-direction will be withdrawn less rapidly from some children than from others, the prospect of this stage need not be alarming. It is only when reorganisation has been too hasty, or when unfavourable conditions have been ignored, that there is much risk of the degree of integration now proposed being unsuccessful.

Since this stage of an integrated programme is not recommended for a class of very young children, it is assumed that they are either family-grouped (with the earlier stages retained for the younger children) or that most of the children are in the second half of their time in the infant school. It is assumed also that the classroom is well organised, and assignment cards are recognisably graded and stored where the children can have access to them.

These last assumptions are made, because without good basic organisation of the classroom and without an adequate supply of systematically planned, well-graded and purposeful apparatus, it is virtually impossible for the child to know what he should do unless the teacher continues to tell him. To think in terms of the withdrawal of teacher-direction would therefore be illusory.

Although it is not suggested that the children's activities will now be entirely dependent upon assignment cards, card apparatus will certainly play an important part in their programme, especially in 3R work; so also will self-selection. Whereas at an earlier stage the child might have been told to take a particular green weighing card, the only instruction he should need now is to 'do some weighing'. He should know which weighing cards apply to his level of attainment, and the system of grading and numbering should be clear enough for him to know which card to do next. This could be assisted by means of a brief record on the inside cover of his work-book, e.g.

Weighing. Set 2
1 √
2 √
3 √ (Ticked by the teacher as
4 √ each card is marked.)
5 √
6 √
7
8
9
10

The purists would argue that a system such as this is only paying lip-service to the withdrawal of teacher-direction, and that the teacher is still in fact deciding what the child must do. Up to a point, the purists are perfectly right; but it is a very important point indeed. The withdrawal of *obvious* teacher-direction in no sense means that the child should become the teacher. It means that the teacher is still very much responsible for the child's educational programme, but she organises it so that he can make the immediate decision without having to await her instruction every time. This does not belittle the value of delegating the immediate decision to the child. *It gives him responsibility within his capacity to support it, and independence of action within limits which he understands and to which he is entitled.* This is what the Integrated Day is all about. It really is not about transferring an unreasonable burden of choice and decision from the teacher to the child.

So much for the essential background to the introduction of Stage IV; a practical plan is now required based on the assumptions already stated. The teacher might begin by arranging a programme to allow for:

(*a*) Activities which for reasons extraneous to the class must take place at specific times, e.g. radio and television programmes.
(*b*) Activities which the teacher prefers should still take place at particular times, e.g. story, drama, R.I., etc. Most teachers will have certain preferences which come into this category.

The rest of the day would then be devoted to integrated activities, but not necessarily all without teacher-direction. There would be periods of discussion with individual children, with a group, or possibly sometimes with the whole class. These would not always be initiated by the teacher, but they would often be developed by her and tactfully 'encouraged' along intended lines. The teacher would pick up opportunities to use a particular child's interest and extend it to others in the form of a topic to be pursued. She might tell a group to collect information to make a graph, or set a box of shapes before two children and ask them to see what they could find out by measuring and comparing them.

The point here is that integration does not prevent the teacher from teaching, or preclude her from giving the children all sorts of opportunities for learning which they might very well not come upon if left entirely to their own resources of interest and investigation. Some of these avenues can be explored as a result of carefully designed assignment cards, but by no means all of them. So much learning comes from the teacher's skill in making use of spontaneous and semi-spontaneous situations, and it would be absurd to suggest that because it is an Integrated Day she may not 'direct' these situations so that they yield profitable results.

The teacher's plan for the day will therefore be flexible enough to make it possible for all this to go on within the period of integrated activity. However, the plan should also be more specific, and should still set certain tasks. The teacher should estimate what each group might reasonably be expected to accomplish in a day, according to the children's capacity and level of attainment and allowing for both direct teaching and the semi-directed activities just discussed. She then draws up a daily programme for each group, writes it on a large card, and gives it to the group in the morning. The instructions on the card would be very general, e.g. 'Read a book which you like', 'Do some measuring'—it being left to the child to choose his own book and find the appropriate measuring assignment.

The daily programme should include:

(*a*) A reading/writing activity, with time to follow up an interest from which reading and writing may come.
(*b*) A mathematics activity, possibly two for some groups because of the range to be covered.
(*c*) A creative or practical activity, directed or undirected, with plenty of scope for individual preference.
(*d*) Reading for pleasure.

In practice, the divisions are not always as clear-cut as this, because of the overlap of skill and interest in all these areas. Indeed, some of the children's work will be in the nature of a 'Centre of Interest', when 'subject' boundaries will be frequently crossed (but a plea here for a child just to paint if he wants to, without having to paint something connected with a Centre of Interest).

However, as a basic pattern for a plan, it is perhaps a useful guide. In devising the plan for the day, the teacher must still keep an eye on questions of movement and chair-based activity, even use of room space, limitation of numbers on certain tasks, etc. But these considerations are not quite as pressing as they were in the earlier stages, because they tend to even themselves out as the period of integrated activity is lengthened and as the children's area of choice is increased.

In planning her daily programmes, the teacher should aim at covering all the activities that each group should have in the course of a week. She can then use the same basic programmes week after week if she wishes, modified as necessary to take account of the children's progress. Of course, there is no reason at all why she should not move into Stage IV by smaller steps than these if she prefers. The period of integrated activity can be shorter to begin with, and the assignments more limited; and as the organisation becomes securely established the full daily programme can follow. A very considerable degree of integration will then have been achieved.

Concluding Stage IV, there is one minor observation that might be worth making. When much of the day is devoted to integrated activities (interspersed with 'reserved periods' which are required for other purposes), it is sometimes a little difficult to indicate briefly to the children that from now until playtime they are free, more or less, to follow the choices available to them on the daily programme card. In one class the children overcame this difficulty by identifying the period as 'day's work' time (or, more accurately, 'dayswork', enunciated clearly as one word). There was a certain aura of importance about this interesting occupation, since it signified an advanced state of knowledge possessed by no other class in the school. It served its purpose. 'Dayswork' was a serious study. After all, nobody else in the place even knew how to do it!

Stage V

In this final stage of the transition to an integrated programme, 'dayswork' becomes 'weekswork' and integration is complete. The organisational structure has already been established in Stage IV. The teacher has her daily programmes, designed to encompass the integrated activities of a whole week but given to the children in daily doses. All that remains is for these programmes to be distributed over a longer period of time, group by group. To begin with, the red group might be given programmes covering two days. As this change is comfortably absorbed, three programmes could be distributed together. In the meantime, the blue group might move to a two-day ration. In due course, the distribution of 'weekswork' to all groups would be complete, with the exception of any group consisting of backward or very young children. For them, 'dayswork' should be retained indefinitely.

This stage of the transition is not nearly as difficult to put into practice as it may seem. The children are by now so used to the requirements of an integrated organisation, and they are so familiar with the range of activities that they must undertake, that they go fairly naturally through their assignments and tick them off on individual 'weekswork' programmes as each is completed. (By this time, the teacher will find it useful to give each child a copy of the programme applicable to his group.) She certainly has to keep an eye on Andrew and Michael and Kate, who are not above ticking their programmes more in accordance with fiction than with fact. But the teacher after all knows her children, and she is perfectly well aware of which of them are likely to try this optimistic ruse. The same children would try equally hard to get by with the minimum of effort in any form of organisation.

A natural question which arises when integration is fairly complete concerns the child who finishes his week's work early or the one who has still not completed it by Friday afternoon. At first, the teacher must have a policy for both these eventualities. If a child has genuinely completed all his assignments before the end of the week, he will usually welcome the suggestion that he may now return to his own particular interest and spend more time on it, or do some more of the assignments that he likes best. His rate of progress can thereby be accelerated in accordance with his own capacity, and there is no risk of his being bored because the pace of the rest of his group is slower than his.

However, it is possible that despite his generally rapid advance there are one or two areas in which he is not quite certain of his ground. Some of the time could very profitably be used to give him additional teaching in order to resolve his difficulty. This should not be overdone. The child may be discouraged from making the effort which enabled him to complete his assignments early in the first place if he knows he will always have to spend the rest of the week slogging at things he finds difficult. There is, however, an opportunity here for some valuable teaching if the teacher handles it helpfully, and it can give a child a sense of real achievement when he makes progress with a problem he had not fully understood.

With the child whose assignments are still incomplete by the end of the week, there are two possible lines of approach. If the teacher is fairly certain that this has been due to lack of application and effort, she must try to make the child recognise this, and do what she can to make him work harder. She may not be very successful, any more than she would be in any other form of organisation. This, after all, is one of the occupational hazards of teaching, and there is no neat solution peculiar to an Integrated Day. If some judicious pressure is thought to be necessary, then it must be applied. The teacher is doing the child no service if she does not try to train him to make the effort when he must.

The second line of approach is to see whether the assignments are incomplete because the child was carried away by a genuine interest in one of his activities, which left him short of time to accomplish everything else. In this case, he should not be allowed to feel he has in some way failed because he took advantage of one of the benefits of an Integrated Day—the opportunity to follow up a personal interest and develop it to a degree which is not always possible in a more formal organisation. A suggestion that the missed assignments should be dealt with earlier the next week, without an issue being made of it, is all that is usually necessary.

However, if the same assignments are always those which are left to the last and are therefore possibly missed too frequently, the teacher should try to discover the reason for the child's apparent unwillingness to tackle them. It may be that there is a process which he does not entirely understand and so he avoids it. A little extra help may be all that is needed to put this right. Or it may be that the form in which the assignment is presented does not capture the child's interest, and it may well be possible to modify it enough to make it more attractive to him. One of the undoubted advantages of an Integrated Day is that it is so much easier to use an individual and personal approach, and to adjust a child's programme to give him every chance of making the most of it.

In course of time, the boundaries of 'weekswork' become artificial, and they disappear. The activities of one week merge into those of the next and each child works at his own pace on his own programme. He ceases to think of having 'finished' it on Thursday or of being behind the clock on Friday. The programme simply becomes a continuous operation, and though it is still there as a personal guide-line to the child it no longer has, or needs, any particular beginning or end.

The group as a unit still exists, to help the teacher to plan and to estimate what she can expect of children at comparable levels of attainment. But her organisational structure, essential though it is, has become so much a part of everyday life that the children no longer really notice it. They take it for granted; it is the normal framework of their day. Its strength could be measured only by the disintegration which would follow if it were inadvisedly removed.

No discussion of the Integrated Day would be complete without a reference to the burning question which comes to the mind of every teacher concerned with the practical issues of integration. The question is: 'What do you do about the child who does not "choose"?'

There is, of course, a standard textbook answer which everybody knows. It is the one about making the task attractive enough, and the child is then bound to choose to do it. Like most standard answers, it contains a grain of truth. A child *is* more likely to choose an attractive task than an unattractive one. Furthermore, if the classroom is badly arranged, or the class is unruly or disorganised, nobody is likely to choose to do anything very constructive anyway. However, there is much more to the question of the child's choosing than this. Even given all the advantages of a well-equipped classroom, attractive material and assignments, good control and a sound and recognisable organisational structure to support it all, there can still be George who does not choose to engage in anything much except aimless and disruptive play.

Leaving aside the particular problem of the severely disturbed or maladjusted child, whose problem is really something different and present in any form of organisation, there can be only one honest answer to the question of what to do about George: he must be told to sit down and do his sums and not get up until he has finished. Integration or no integration, nothing less will do if George's interests are to be properly served.

Chapter 7

Supplementary Organisation—Integrated and Traditional

IMMEDIATE ADAPTATION BY THE TEACHER TO AN INTEGRATED DAY

Strong though the case may be for children to move gradually from a traditional to an integrated organisation, a teacher will have to make the change immediately if she goes to a school where an Integrated Day is already operating. Yet the circumstances are very different from those which apply if a class of children is suddenly changed from one to the other. The teacher goes to an established situation. The children are already used to integration; the school is geared to it; and help and advice are available from the Head and from colleagues to assist the new teacher until she becomes familiar with a different way of organising and teaching her class.

However, neither Head nor colleagues can be with her all the time, and though they may do a great deal to acquaint her with the details of the organisation in that particular school, she will be on her own with the children for much of the time. She must accept the new pattern from her first day, and it is important that she should be sufficiently confident not to appear uncertain to the children or to feel hesitant in her approach to an unfamiliar set of circumstances.

Even if she takes over a really well organised class, she must prepare herself to meet her new commitments. The organisation may be strong enough for the children to continue with a programme which is almost second nature to them; and this will give the teacher the opportunity to observe and absorb the detail of what goes on, so that she can build her own plans around the established system. However, children being children, it is optimistic to suppose that there will be no more to it than this. Despite the strength of the existing structure, the opportunity for some of the more tumultuous inhabitants of the class to try something different on a new teacher may be too good to miss.

Has any teacher heard anything more convincing than the assurances of the butter-wouldn't-melt-in-his-mouth character? 'But Miss, we *always* play rockets now. Miss Williams said so!' In the absence of any evidence that Miss Williams possessed a pair of ear-plugs, the new teacher is justified in insisting upon an alternative occupation with a more conspicuous educational purpose. However, she can do this to much greater effect if she can offer three positive alternatives to the forbidden rockets. Here is the first essential item of her preparations.

Having acquainted herself in advance with some of the detail of the children's normal routine and the activities which they usually undertake, she should have about half a dozen 'suggestions' up her sleeve, and the materials required to carry them out, to meet just such a contingency. Apart from the rocket addicts, there may also be other children who in due course leave the activity on which they are engaged and are uncertain about what to do next. However effective Miss Williams' organisation may have been, the very fact of there being a new teacher is itself sometimes enough to make children a little unsure of their direction. A positive approach by the new teacher, who seems to know what she wants and who makes available a few promising activities, does much to help the children if in the unfamiliar situation their momentum threatens to give out.

Another useful contribution to the teacher's preparations for the first few days is for her to have in reserve some class and group activities of varying length to which she can turn at short notice if she feels the need to do so. With children whom she does not yet know and a new form of organisation as well, she may find that a short united effort now and again helps to prevent the class from becoming too diversified. The individual approach which is one of the advantages of an Integrated Day will not be threatened if the teacher allows herself (and the children) the reassurance of some directed activity of this kind, as long as it is not overdone and does not cut across any sustained individual effort which some children may be making at the time.

These positive occupational plans, together with the established programme with which the teacher will make herself familiar as soon as possible, will help her over the first few days while she and the children are becoming acquainted with each other. Since at this stage she will wish to retain as far as possible the organisation that is already there, the teacher will find out about any grouping pattern which exists and the capacities of the children within the groups. If the class is not organised in immediately distinguishable groups, she must manage without them for the moment. If no specific daily programme is inherited from the previous teacher, she must plan from day to day on the basis of her observation of the children and such information as is available to her from records or any other source.

The pattern of a well organised class will emerge very quickly even if it is not directly apparent in the first day or two. The new teacher will learn a great deal from it, and not least from the children themselves as soon as they know her and respect her. She is bound to want to do some things differently, for after all no two teachers work in exactly the same way. But her changes can come gradually, and in a favourable situation it will be some time before they are likely to amount to much more than those needed to reflect her personal techniques. The children will have little difficulty in absorbing them without being unduly disturbed.

If, however, the existing organisation is not as strong as it might be and a new teacher, despite her inexperience of an Integrated Day, is aware of a need for rather more extensive change, she will have to move cautiously. She might make the children even more unsettled by being too precipitate. Her first step is to consult the Head, explain the problem, and put forward some constructive proposals for dealing with it. The Head's experience and advice will not only help her with her plans, but will safeguard her from making changes which might run counter to the established policy of the school.

It may be advisable, if the Head agrees, to formalise the organisation slightly for a temporary period. The teacher must use this time to gain the children's confidence, and she can then ease them rather than press them into doing things differently. She can enlist their help in reorganising the classroom, as long as she does not remove the familiar landmarks all at once. She can plan her grouping system and her daily programmes, building as much as she can on any existing organisational features which she can use. She can then bring in her changes by reshaping here and modifying there, rather than by sweeping away all at once an organisation which at least is familiar even if it has weaknesses. As long as the teacher is prepared to plan carefully, to make intelligent use of the established structure as much as she can and to adapt herself to it as she goes along, she will assimilate the organisation of the Integrated Day while helping to strengthen it with her own personal contribution.

RECORDS

Records can be time-consuming to keep, and if they are very detailed, excessively burdensome. Sometimes the teacher has to spend so long on them that she wonders whether there is anything whatever to be gained from the exercise. The extreme view is that if it is all satisfactorily in the teacher's head, there is no point in putting it down on paper anyway.

If no records are kept, however, significant gaps in the children's essential activities can in certain circumstances go unnoticed for too long. With a large class, it is not really possible to remember that Willie weighed on Wednesday and that James has not opened his reading-book for more than a week. Every bit of detail is not necessarily of value; but some of it is, and the human memory is fallible. It therefore has to be supplemented by records.

On the other hand, the teacher's knowledge of her children is more valuable in some respects than a minutely itemised catalogue of each child's work. One of the arguments used in support of very detailed records is that they are necessary 'in case the teacher is away and a supply has to take over'. This argument is not as convincing as it sounds. In the first place, the 'supply' will probably not look at them anyway; and secondly, even if she did they would not tell her what she really needs to know about Linda's reading difficulties, though the teacher knows them as well as she knows Linda. So a balance must be found between records which are full enough to keep account of what really needs to be known about each child, and those which are so detailed that they irritate the teacher and make little positive contribution to her work with the class.

It is so often assumed that records are kept only by the teacher that it is easy to overlook the value of those in which the children play a part. For example, with a reading record most teachers probably adopt the well-tried system of writing on a manilla book-marker the number of the last page the child has read. This is an excellent practice. It shows Karen that she has reached the end of page 18. It gives her a sense of achievement to see the numbers growing larger and to know that she will soon have another reading-book. In addition, the teacher has to look no further than Karen's book-marker to find the right page when she hears her read, and it is a system which has always seemed to work very satisfactorily all round.

But is it really necessary for the teacher to duplicate the same information in her own record book? Admittedly there is the awful possibility that Karen might one day lose her book-marker; and the exact page she had reached might never be accurately known. Karen would have a pretty good idea that she had reached page 18, but if she were a page or two out how much, in all seriousness, would it matter?

The only reading record which the teacher needs to keep is a note of the day on which she hears Karen read. This is necessary in order to make sure that the child reads to her often enough, and that all the children read to her in turn. A record of this nature, however, requires no more than a tick in a column headed '21st', which can be done while the child is reading and no more time has to be spent on it at all.

For mathematics the position is different because of the variety of mathematical activities in which the child may engage. With some of them, where there can be a system of grading with numbered cards, the record on the inside cover of each child's work-book as suggested on page 71 is worth considering. The child has the advantage of knowing what he has done and what he should do next, and this information is available to the teacher at any time that she needs it. The additional value of having it duplicated in her own record book is so marginal that it does not compensate for the time she would have to spend on putting it there.

To keep a check on when John measures, as opposed to what kind of measuring he is doing, the teacher can, with group work in a traditional programme, devise a simple system which requires a minimum of time to operate. Her record book for a group would read as follows:

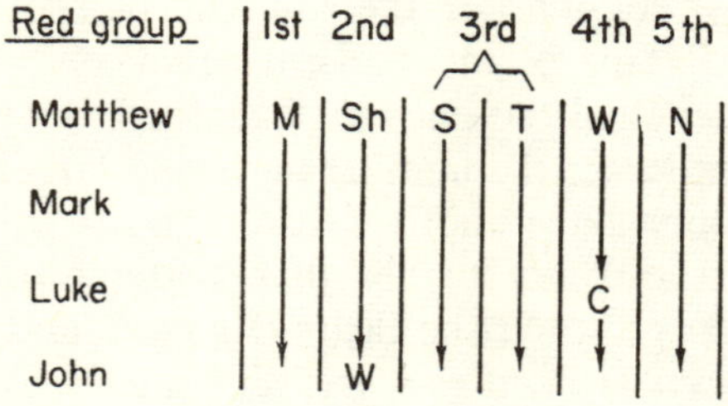

Key: M – measuring; Sh – shopping; S – sums; T – time; W – water-play; N – number; C – creative activity; or whatever divisions and symbols the teacher prefers.

A similar record can, if the teacher wishes, be kept in an Integrated Day, though the entries must be individual and they take longer. If the child has reached the stage when most of his recording is written, the easiest time to make the entry is when marking his work; otherwise the teacher must do it when she sees the child engaged on that activity.

However, it must be remembered that with an Integrated Day organisation, if the children are working to daily or weekly programmes, the programmes themselves provide a good record of the tasks they accomplish. With these, and the records in the children's own work-books, very little additional detail should have to be recorded by the teacher. In this situation her records can, in most cases, be limited to little more than the highlights of a child's progress; when, for example, Timothy in the green group reaches the stage when he can move on to the blue group's programme. This matters, because it affects his future assignments; and it is a milestone which the teacher will find it useful to record.

It is in the reception class, or with very young children in any class, that the teacher's written records need to be more extensive, because the 'assignments' which are suitable for recording in the children's own work-books are fewer. Yet even here the teacher's records do not always need to be as detailed as they sometimes are. Once again, it is the highlights which really matter. If, for example, Jill is 'playing' with practical mathematical apparatus from which she is learning her number values, only the fact needs to be recorded; and this can quite quickly be done with the type of teacher's record already suggested, a symbol in a dated column. The significant step to note is when Jill really knows her number values, or grasps conservation, because then a new range of activities is open to her.

The most important function of a teacher's record book is that it should show the highlights and draw attention to the gaps; and this function should be fulfilled by the simplest and quickest means. The teacher's book should never duplicate information contained on children's book-markers or in their work-books, where it can often be of more value than in a book which children never see. Record-keeping is nearly always a chore; but it need not necessarily be a burden. If it is a burden, then too many records are being kept. It is time to look at the record book and see how much of the detail is really necessary.

HEARING READING

It is probable that no infant teacher, unless she has an unusually small class, ever solves the problem of hearing reading entirely to her satisfaction. It has for so long been a maxim that she must hear all her children read every day that at first she hardly dares to confess how far she usually is from achieving this desirable objective. It seems to her that every other teacher must be managing it perfectly well—and of course her own class will in consequence suffer the most dreadful disabilities because of her miserable incompetence.

Like never losing her patience with Peter when he spits, hearing all her children read every day is a splendid educational dictum. Unfortunately, however, the sheer mathematics of the thing often makes it impossible. If there are thirty-five children in the class, and a ration of three minutes is allowed for each child, the teacher must spend an hour and three-quarters out of a total teaching day of about four hours (excluding assembly, milk, playtime, dinner, etc.) in doing virtually nothing except hearing children read. When, we may ask, does she teach them to read in order that she can hear them?

It is true, of course, that the infant teacher quite soon cultivates the ability to hear a child read and attend momentarily to something else at the same time; but even this has its limits. The only other way to hear children read every day is to hear them in groups, with each child reading two or three sentences while the others allegedly follow what is going on. Fortunately this practice is dying out, because of its mechanical nature and its lack of attention to the individual child. A teacher may still be driven to it because of particularly difficult circumstances, but educationally it is a poor alternative to hearing each child separately. What, then, is a realistic and sensible policy at which to aim?

There are two possible ways of arranging to hear children read individually:

1. A child may read to the teacher at any time during the day while the class is busy on all manner of other activities. In an odd few minutes, when the teacher is not directly engaged on something which claims most of her attention, she will fit in one or two readers. This is a common practice, and it works reasonably well. There are ways, however, of helping it to work a little better:

(*a*) The teacher must set herself a goal, or she may find that at the end of the day she has hardly heard anyone read at all. She may not reach this goal, but it is still important to set it. She therefore decides which group or groups she will try to hear that day.

(*b*) She tells the children in one of these groups to take out their reading-books and have them ready. This can be quite a time-saving device. By the time Geoffrey searches out his book, drops his book-marker twice on the way, trips over the bag of bricks and stops to pass the time of day with David, several precious minutes have gone by during which the teacher might have been hearing him read. If the book is at hand, it can make an appreciable difference.

(*c*) The teacher then goes round this group, hearing two or three children read when the opportunity arises and returning to the rest when she can; alternatively she calls a child to her when the moment is there. It is often quicker to take the first of these alternatives.

(*d*) When she has heard all these children, she does the same thing with the next group; and so she hears as many readers as she can in the course of the day.

2. With older infants, a 'reading time' can be set aside each day, when every child in the class has a book to read or to look through. It need not necessarily be his reading-book; in fact it is quite a good thing if it is not, because it encourages him to read books other than those in the reading schemes. There is something to be said for having this period immediately after a break; as the children return to the classroom they choose a book and thus do not crowd into the bays all at the same moment.

The children whom the teacher intends to hear during this period are told to collect their reading-books in addition to the book of their choice, and she goes round them or calls them to her as she prefers. This period should not go on for more than about ten minutes or so, or the children will become restive. However, it is long enough for the teacher to hear three or four readers while the rest of the class is engaged reasonably quietly on something really profitable.

This alternative cannot be used instead of the first, because it will not enable the teacher to hear enough children for the day; but it is a useful additional time for hearing reading, and with older infants the reading period has its merits.

If, by these expedients, the teacher can hear twelve to fifteen children read in a day she is doing very well indeed. Her task is easier if she has an 'infant helper' for part of the week; but she should herself hear every child in turn, arranging a rotation with the helper to make this possible.

It is better to hear a child read properly once in two or three days, than ostensibly to hear him read every day, cursorily and only half attentively because of lack of time. There is no doubt that it is essential for every child to read *something* every day: from books in the various bays, from apparatus and assignment cards, from the blackboard or from charts; and some of this they will read to the teacher in the natural course of events. However, they cannot necessarily read to her every day from their reading-books, and to overlook the importance of other kinds of reading is to elevate the reading scheme to an unnatural status. The teacher must certainly hear the children read; but she must also have time to teach them to do so.

MARKING

There is a tendency to believe that all marking of infants' work must be done in their presence, because by the next day it will mean nothing to them. With very young children this is certainly true; yesterday's affairs have faded and become quite irrelevant by today. But with these children the problem is not a considerable one for the teacher. Their output of written material which requires 'marking' is generally small; and marking usually consists of a word or two of discussion about what they have done, and perhaps a tick which pleases the child and is regarded somehow as the official seal of approval on the effort he has made.

As children progress through the infant school, however, their written recording increases rapidly; and by the time they reach the top infant year the volume of work to be marked is far greater than the teacher can possibly deal with in the presence of each child. It is a bit like hearing reading. If the teacher conscientiously strives for the ideal she is defeated by time, and very important areas of her teaching are inevitably neglected.

Fortunately children can, by this time, review their written work of the day before and consider the implications of any comment or correction which the teacher has made. They are quite capable of seeing Monday's work in Tuesday's setting. It is therefore possible for the teacher to mark when the children are not there and return their books in time for the next day's programme. If her day permits her to deal sometimes with a child's work in his presence this can be helpful, especially if he is experiencing some particular difficulty. Generally speaking, however, it is better to mark the bulk of it afterwards. It is far more valuable for a teacher to spend her time in teaching, in the broad sense of the word, than on a perpetual journey round the class with pencil in hand and a desperate eye on the clock.

As the children reach the stage when their marking can be done later, it is advisable to institute some kind of system which they know and use. Without this, every book will end up in haphazard confusion on the teacher's desk, along with Simon's missing pistol and the motley collection of odds and ends which have found their way there in the course of the day. A 'marking box' is extremely useful. All work for marking is put in this box as it is completed, and although some insistence is necessary to ensure that everyone uses it there is no great difficulty in training children to accept it as a matter of course.

If they have been working from assignment cards, the cards themselves should be handed in as well, inside the books. Without them, the answers can be quite meaningless to the teacher unless the children are required to record many more words than the activity justifies. Cards and books can then be returned to their places in readiness for the next day, and really with a class of infants the whole operation does not take very long.

There is one minor problem which can arise, especially with an Integrated Day when children are pursuing a whole range of different assignments in accordance with their separate programmes. It can happen that a child engages in something which he evidently does not fully understand, but this does not emerge until he has written it down, consigned it to the marking box and gone home. The teacher then realises that he needs some help to put it right, or the same mistake will be repeated and the child's progress hindered. In an Integrated Day the teacher cannot be certain when he will choose to come round to that activity again and she may miss the opportunity of resolving his difficulty.

There is a very simple answer to this which works well. An agreed symbol is used—perhaps a blue apple or a red square—and if this appears on the page the child knows that he must take it to the teacher and find out what is wrong. She is then reminded of the need to help him, and misunderstandings are not perpetuated. Children are not unwilling to conform to this arrangement if it is part of their accepted organisation and they are used to it. Once again, the teacher knows if there are any who are likely to ignore her apples and squares and, as in many other things, she has to resort to more direct methods with these children.

A simple and sensible system for collecting work to be marked helps the teacher's organisation to work well. It is an example of how a systematic approach to a comparatively small item of class management can strengthen the main structure, and it is often in these areas of 'supplementary' organisation that minor snags can be eliminated before they become troublesome or even just mildly irritating.

Chapter 8

The Organisation of School Classes

It is now so rare to find the classes in an infant school organised on the basis of streaming by ability that fortunately there is no need to consider it as a practical possibility. Except in very small schools, however, there has to be an alternative policy for dividing the children among the classes, and there are three methods by which this is most commonly done:

(i) Single-age grouping.
(ii) Family or vertical grouping.
(iii) Parallel grouping.

SINGLE-AGE GROUPING

On the whole, an organisation based on single-age grouping is probably still the most widely used: that is to say, the classes are divided according to the age of the children. The age range in any one class may be just a few months or it may be nearly a year, depending upon the numbers in the school and the size of its annual reception class intake. One of the effects of organising a school in this way is that the children fall within a narrower band of intellectual, social, emotional and physical development than they do if the full age range of the infant school is represented within one class.

This is not to say that there cannot be a fairly considerable difference in the ability and the maturity of children who are of roughly comparable chronological age. The differences can be very marked, and the variation in their rates of progress appreciable; but these variations are generally greater if there is in addition a difference of two to three years in the children's ages.

However, despite the benefits of a narrower range for teaching and for the provision of classroom material and equipment, single-age grouping has its disadvantages as well. The task of the reception class teacher, in particular, is not an easy one. In a large school, situated in an area in which there is a high proportion of families with young children, there may be a full class of about forty new entrants all beginning at the same time. These children come together to the unfamiliar world of school, and many of them have had little or no experience of sharing the time and attention of one adult with others in so large a group. In this new, and to some children frighteningly large, situation of people and things, the child's overwhelming need is for attention and for personal contact with the teacher to help him over the early strangeness and unfamiliarity of school life. Yet it is this very attention which it is difficult for the teacher to provide when there are so many children in need of it at the same moment.

The reception class teacher's problems do not end with satisfying the children's need for security and emotional stability as they settle in to school; or indeed with organising their daily programme so that they learn and make progress. There are the practical matters, like sorting out forty pairs of almost identical wellingtons, so that the right and left boots reach, if possible, the right and left feet of their lawful owners. (And of course it is imperative that the teacher should have mastered the technique of untying the tightest possible knots in an infinite number of shoe laces, after they have failed to respond to preliminary treatment by chewing.)

The increasing use of auxiliary staff in infant schools is invaluable to the teacher of very young children and does much to help her with the day-to-day affairs of her reception class. But the organisational and practical problems inherent in a large class of new entrants, all bewildered together, all comparatively unskilled, continue to be extremely pressing despite the welcome assistance of another pair of hands.

It is not, however, only within the walls of the reception class that single-age grouping presents its difficulties. They appear also in the organisation of the school itself, and they arise because of the practice of termly admission at the beginning of the infant school and only annual transfer to the junior school at the end of it. This means that a large infant school opens with smaller numbers in September, fills up rapidly during the year and is almost bursting at the seams in the summer term. With single-age grouping in this situation a teacher is needed for a full new class each term; and there is no easy way of arranging it with a permanent staffing ratio which is usually calculated on the basis of average numbers throughout the year.

There are two main alternatives open to the Head in deciding how to organise the classes in these circumstances:

1. There may be one member of the staff who by choice always takes the reception class and keeps the children for their introductory term while they are settling in to school. All the other classes are divided, according to age, among the remaining teachers. At the beginning of their second term, most of the children from the reception class move up to the next one in order that the new entrants may be accommodated; and throughout the school groups of children move up, usually on an age basis, so that all classes absorb the extra numbers occasioned by the new intake.

This is a fairly simple form of organisation and it has the merit of enabling all classes to be smaller in size in the September term while all share equally the increased numbers during the year. Its main defect—and it is a major one—is that there is, unavoidably, a great deal of movement between classes. If to this movement is added a different class teacher each September as classes change hands, and more changes when new teachers replace any who leave, some children can have so many teachers on their way through the infant school that their progress suffers because of the lack of continuity in their teaching.

2. An alternative is to have all the classes larger in September, keeping one teacher without a class of her own to do remedial work throughout the school for that term. She is then available to take the class of new entrants in January and no movement of children between classes is necessary. For the new intake in

the summer, a temporary teacher may be taken on the staff for the one term, or if this is not possible a 'general post' has to take place as in the first alternative.

This method slightly reduces the number of changes a child might have; but the problem of recruiting an additional member of staff for the summer term can sometimes be solved —if it can be solved at all—only by taking on two part-time teachers, which is not really very satisfactory for children of infant school age. It is in the summer term, when the numbers are at their peak in all infant schools, that the demand for extra help is at its height and additional teachers are very hard to find.

Some slight variation is possible on either of these two ways of organising classes with single-age grouping, but all of them present similar problems of movement between classes as the school fills up from below during the year. There is no really satisfactory answer to this except for one modification which can go a long way towards reducing the number of teacher changes a child may have. This is for a teacher to take a term's new entrants and to 'move up' with the main body of her class as they go through the school, staying with them until they eventually leave. This system does not entirely avoid teacher changes, because a certain amount of movement from a class to the one above may still be necessary to accommodate increasing numbers during the year; but the changes of teacher for any one child are far fewer than in the traditional system in which a class always has a new teacher at the beginning of each school year.

This is a tradition which, with single-age grouping, is very generally followed, but there is a good deal to be said for breaking with it in order to give the children greater continuity of teaching. So much of the success of a teacher's classroom organisation depends upon the children's familiarity with it, that their progress is slightly slowed down each time they have to adjust to the different ways of another teacher; and if the teacher has the same class from year to year she can build on her early training of the children and take full advantage of its effects. Continuity is particularly important with an Integrated Day, for here familiarity with the detailed organisation is crucial. In any form of organisation, however, teacher and children can do so much more if they know each other really well, and in considering single-age grouping it should not be assumed that an annual teacher change is essential. Indeed, without this change one of its greatest disadvantages is so much reduced that it bears more favourable comparison, in certain circumstances, with other ways of organising classes in an infant school.

FAMILY GROUPING

In a family-grouped organisation, every class contains the full age and ability range of the infant school. All classes are identical in structure, and families and friends can stay together unless there are reasons in a particular case that would make this undesirable. There is, of course, no reception class as such. Each class throughout the school receives an equal number of new entrants every term, so that even with a large new intake no teacher ever has more than a few children who are just starting school. Once a year, all classes lose roughly the same number of seven-year-olds to the junior school.

The principle has long been established in small country schools, which have always been family-grouped by force of circumstances. Indeed, family grouping was first introduced to urban classes by teachers who had become convinced of its benefits by their experience in rural areas, and who were concerned to extend these benefits to children in the towns. In town schools, however, classes are likely to be much bigger; and it is the combination of large numbers and the extensive age and ability range of a family-grouped class which often leads to the choice of a single-age structure.

For the child, the theoretical advantages of family grouping are substantial. When he first starts school he comes into a class in which there might be an older brother or sister, or even an older friend, who provides a comforting link with the world of home. The older child can help the younger one to feel less strange in his new surroundings, and can give him some of the extra attention and practical assistance he needs until he has settled down. The benefit to the older children comes from the development of qualities of leadership and responsibility, in acting on behalf of the teacher in many ways and in showing consideration to those who are less mature and less skilful than themselves.

Children learn a great deal from each other, and this can be to the advantage of some of the older as well as the younger ones. The older child can strengthen a half-established concept by helping a younger friend to grasp it, and a backward child in a class containing those much younger than himself has many opportunities for going back to an earlier stage with less sense of failure—he is doing it 'to help Jennifer'. The younger children, on the other hand, can learn of intellectual possibilities from contact with those who are more advanced—in developing their interests, in pursuing creative activities, in using books and from conversation with each other. Inter-age group activity in the classroom and in the playground is valuable for social and intellectual reasons, and children in quite a wide age range have much to gain from shared experience and from having natural daily contact in a variety of learning situations.

As far as the children and their learning are concerned, these are some of the theoretical justifications for family grouping. In practice it does not always work out quite like this, but the advantages are certainly there some of the time and children do benefit from the contribution that those older or younger than themselves can make. It would, however, be idle to pretend that there are no difficulties. If the older children are given too much responsibility for helping the younger ones, they can find it troublesome and distracting and it can hold them back. Furthermore, it is not particularly unusual for brothers and sisters to be happier in separate classes. They are together at home, and they can be stimulated and refreshed by being independent of each other at school. Again, 'helping Janet' or 'learning from Robert' can provide a heaven-sent opportunity for avoiding something else, and it would be remarkable if every chance to do nothing much quite legitimately were virtuously ignored.

However, these reservations do not invalidate the benefits of family grouping. Situations of this kind are part of a teacher's life, and no form of school organisation is free of all problems. But to ignore their existence is to be unrealistic, and in acknowledging that they are there the teacher may anticipate and avoid them.

She may also take heart from the knowledge that a family-grouped class, if it is well organised, can offer her other advantages. After the first time, she is not again presented with an entire class that is new to her. She always has a nucleus of children, trained in the detail of her class organisation, who keep it going while newcomers absorb it. This is an immense help, for children who are confident in a familiar situation very quickly transmit to others the pattern of the daily routine. The teacher is also in the fortunate position of being able to have her children long enough to know them, and their parents, really very well. This is possible without family grouping; but with it, it is inevitable. It can be very satisfying to see the extent of a child's progress between his first day in the infant school and his last. The view can never be as long if the child is with the teacher for only part of that time.

However, the wide range of ability and interest in a family-grouped class calls for a rather different approach in some respects from that which is appropriate to single-age grouping. Group teaching is possible for most children when they are fairly close in age and in their degree of maturity, and as long as the teacher makes special provision for those at either extreme of the ability range, with some individual teaching where this is necessary, she can meet without too much difficulty the needs of all her children. With family grouping a certain amount of group teaching is possible; but the groups will be smaller and there will be more of them, and this must be taken into account with organisational plans. However, much more individual teaching is essential if family grouping is to be really successful.

For this reason, teaching a family-grouped class is in many ways easier where an Integrated Day is in operation. It follows that if conditions are unfavourable to integration, family grouping should be carefully considered before it is introduced, especially where classes are large. It is by no means impossible, without integration, to manage the degree of individual teaching which family grouping requires; but it does need skill and really good organisation on the part of the teacher if it is to work well.

One other area in which some adjustment is necessary for family grouping is in anything which involves the whole class, such as stories and poetry. A story or poem which satisfies the seven-year-old may be quite without interest for the very young child, and vice versa. It is therefore preferable either to present these on a group basis, or to make an arrangement with the teacher of another class whereby each plans stories and poems at different levels of interest and the children from both classes join whichever they prefer.

From the point of view of overall school organisation, the great merit of family grouping is that it entirely solves the problem of accommodating new entrants termly without having to move children from one class to another during the year. On the other hand, the extensive provision of material and equipment that is necessary to encompass the full age and ability range in every class can be quite a serious drawback. Apart from being expensive this is sometimes impracticable in very small rooms. If the only way round it is to make insufficient provision for all the children in the class, then the advisability of introducing family grouping in that school is in question. Like almost everything else in infant school organisation, a pattern which is eminently successful in some circumstances is not necessarily appropriate to all others. Discrimination and judgement are needed to select that which in the conditions of a particular school is likely to be the best.

PARALLEL GROUPING

There is a compromise between the single-age and the family-grouped class which is generally described as 'parallel grouping'. The term is sometimes applied to any form of organisation in which there are identically structured parallel classes, but in this particular context it is used, for want of a better form of words, to denote a specific arrangement of ages in the infant school.

It is the organisation in which the infant age range is divided half-way up, which is at a chronological age of about six.

Above and below this age, the children are in parallel classes, and each class of older children is loosely paired with a younger one. For example, in a two-form entry infant school with six classes, the arrangement would be:

$$\text{Class} \quad \frac{\text{A} \quad \text{B} \quad \text{C}}{\text{D} \quad \text{E} \quad \text{F}}$$

Classes A, B and C have, divided equally between them, all the children in the upper half of the age range; D, E and F have all those in the lower half. Each class has its own teacher, and each child belongs to his own class; but there is a good deal of contact and interchange between each pair. A child in class D might go one afternoon to class A to join in an activity in which he happens to have a real interest. The teachers might take each other's class for a story, or perhaps for music in which one has a particular strength. Thus there is communication between the two classes, and the teachers are well known to the children in both.

New entrants are admitted equally to classes D, E and F, and some of their oldest children are then transferred to the upper class of the pair in order to keep the numbers balanced. In this way no child normally has more than two teachers while he is in the infant school, and the second of these is already quite well known to him before he moves into her class. Neither teacher ever loses her whole class at the same time, so she retains some of the benefits of having children who know her routine and can help others to become familiar with it.

Parallel grouping in this form has many of the advantages of family grouping, and it avoids certain of the drawbacks of the single-age class: there is some social and intellectual contact between children of different ages; families and friends can be in paired classes, so there can fairly easily be communication between them when this is helpful; there is a degree of continuity for teachers as well as children, which can be mutually beneficial; and there is no serious organisational problem of accommodating new entrants or of causing excessive movement between classes at the beginning of every term.

If, therefore, circumstances are such that the full age range of family grouping is thought to be inadvisable, parallel grouping on these lines might be a workable alternative to the single-age structure. As it is a form of organisation which comes half-way between the other two, it does not have the full advantages—nor all the difficulties—of either. It has, however, merits of its own which are not inconsiderable; and it may be worth looking at if the family or single-age grouping in a school is for any reason under review.

Chapter 9

Team Teaching

In recent years, schools in some areas have been moving towards a form of organisation which breaks away from the class as a teaching unit. 'Team teaching' or 'co-operative teaching' as an alternative to the traditional system is being tried out in a number of different ways. The general principle underlying this movement is that children profit from the variety of skill and expertise that a team, as opposed to only one teacher, can make available to them; and that teachers can gain from co-operating in a joint venture with children, the experienced supporting the inexperienced, and the particular strength of each being used for the benefit of all.

The Plowden Report comments: 'Most primary school work is done in classes. The children who form a class spend most of the day with their class teacher. This is what teachers are used to and what overwhelmingly they think right.'[1]

But: '. . . In making a case for children to have experience of individual, group and class work are we merely justifying what exists? Are the class and the class teacher necessary? Supporters of "team teaching", a method developed in the USA, raise this question.'[2]

There is probably not yet enough evidence for or against the results of team teaching in this country to draw conclusions which can have general application over a wide field of infant teaching. But since we are fortunate enough to enjoy an educational system which allows us to try out, in our schools, different methods and ideas, we have the opportunity of observing some of the ways in which team teaching is now

[1] Plowden Report, H.M.S.O., 1967, para. 752.

[2] Ibid., para. 761.

developing. There is no set formula, and no great uniformity of experiment. There are, however, certain broad lines of advance which have gone far enough to bear examination and comment.

Allowing for the variety of detail found in individual infant schools, team teaching is most commonly organised in one of three ways:

1. Classes are paired and each pair becomes one working unit. (Sometimes this is extended to include three classes.) If the classrooms adjoin, part or all of the connecting wall may be removed. Each teacher is responsible for one 'class', for registration and for the children's welfare, and each has her base in her own classroom area. The teachers work together, and each offers, in co-operation with the other, different activities or the same activity at a different level, or sometimes an alternative approach which might appeal to some children. For example, one may for three weeks or so be specialising in a particular approach to mathematics; the second may be following up a project and developing reading and writing and perhaps other interests from it. One teacher may be musical, the other artistic, and they co-operate to use these talents for the benefit of the children in both classes.

The children use the area of the two classrooms quite freely and pursue their own interests with whatever is being offered by either teacher. Some duplication of equipment is necessary because of numbers, but in certain cases one item is sufficient for all the children and the saving can go towards increased provision of something else.

Occasionally the organisation is completely unstructured, activities being left entirely to the undirected choice of the children. More often, however, there is a good deal of structuring and each teacher follows fairly closely what the children in her 'class' are doing. She designs a programme for them, and sees that they all 'choose', at some time, to undertake the activities which the programme requires.

The success of this arrangement is usually closely related to the skill and experience—and the conviction—of the teachers concerned, and to the degree of planning which supports the children's programme. This, of course, is true in any kind of organisation, but for obvious reasons the demands on the teachers in this situation are exacting. Any weakness in organising ability or control or capacity to co-operate comes under greater strain than it does in a more self-contained approach; and if the children's day is completely unstructured, it is very difficult for them to know what their objectives are. The organisation can therefore present the most pressing problems unless it is clearly planned and developed, and the planning must naturally be the result of extensive consultation between the teachers or there will be gaps and duplication of effort. If, however, the teachers work well together and each really knows what their joint effort is intended to achieve, they can find the co-operation and the companionship most satisfying. Teachers who have worked successfully together in this way often express great unwillingness to return to the isolation of their own separate classrooms.

2. Two or three classes are combined for teaching purposes and each classroom is turned into a 'workshop' room or base for one or more activities. For example, three rooms might become areas for mathematics, language and creative arts. One teacher stays in each, perhaps for a whole morning or an afternoon, and plans for that one activity a programme which caters for the full age and ability range of the three classes. The children go to each room, perhaps by individual choice, but preferably according to a prepared scheme which aims at ensuring that they cover all the activities they should. Under such a scheme, the children are usually divided into groups which for a variety of reasons may well cut across their 'class' grouping. Sometimes the groups move round to the different activities at more or less specified intervals, in order to avoid overcrowding in any one area and to make it easier for the teachers to know what each child has done. The teachers also move round so that they are not committed to only one activity all the time.

This pattern is sometimes used in schools where it is not possible to connect classrooms with each other by the removal of doors or party walls. Once again, co-operative planning and careful record-keeping are essential if the organisation is to function efficiently with so many children.

3. An 'open-plan' system is adopted, where the construction of the school makes this possible. The children and the teachers from several classes move freely over the combined classroom space, and certain activities or stages of activities are developed in particular areas or bays established for the purpose. Any teacher will be responsible for one or more areas for a certain period of time as part of a pre-arranged plan which the teachers in the team constantly work out as they go along.

There may, for example, be a bay where a teacher is developing a theme about shapes which she estimates may need two or three weeks. At the same time she will probably be responsible for adjacent areas in which there are activities unconnected with her theme but to which she attends. Children move about to the bays or corners where different things are going on at their own level, and so their personal interests and progress are sustained by the variety of provision and by the momentum which such a system, if it is working well, generates.

Where, however, it does work really well the children's programme is structured, perhaps unobtrusively, but nevertheless very efficiently indeed. Each child has his own teacher, who is his immediate point of contact and whom he recognises as being responsible for him. The children also have a home bay which is known to be theirs and in which they may start and finish the day. They may all return to it at intervals, with their own teacher, and some kind of class activity such as poetry or a story takes place. The teacher keeps in close touch with her children during the day, wherever they are. She requires them to undertake any tasks that are being neglected, and she takes groups for direct teaching as she considers necessary. This is possible because the children become so used to working on their own or in groups that they can be left to continue while the teacher deals directly with another group.

It is clear that the planning and organisation required of the teachers in this situation must be of a high order. It all has to be undertaken outside school hours, and it presupposes a full contribution from every member of the team if others are not to be overloaded or diverted from their purposes to repair weaknesses in the structure. It is, however, very successfully done in some schools. New members of staff have the opportunity to learn from those who are already experienced in the detail of the organisation, and as auxiliary help is fully integrated into the work of the team it is possible to make the most constructive use of all the adult help that is available.

Children in any form of team-teaching organisation nearly always have a home base of some kind and a teacher who is identified as 'theirs'. These arrangements are important in order to give the young child a sense of belonging to a manageably small part of a large group and a secure relationship with one adult who has, for him, a personal concern. In the course of a day, he will also have a good deal of contact with all the other teachers in the team, and he will himself be part of the co-operative, collective atmosphere which is distinctive of team teaching.

It is sometimes argued that this collective approach, and consequently the number of different teachers with whom the child is involved, makes impossible the continuity and the steady relationship with one teacher which are so important at the infant school stage. The supporters of team teaching, however, are unconvinced by this argument. They maintain that there is, or can be, one teacher in the team whom the child acknowledges as his, and this can give him enough of the stability of a personal relationship to satisfy his need. Furthermore, they believe that a child is stimulated by contact with more than one adult, and that even young children can be very happy in a situation in which they come to know several adults really well.

This is not, of course, an exact reversal of the view that it is unsettling for children to suffer too many changes of teacher on their way through the infant school. It is really a different situation altogether. With team teaching, the child knows and is used to working with several adults from the beginning. By and large, these will still be the same adults when he reaches the end of the infant school. Staff changes, or team changes, will have brought in some new faces; but the child can adapt more easily to these, because the other faces in the team are still those which are well-tried and familiar. It is more difficult when the one and only class teacher changes too frequently, for the change is then almost total. In team teaching, it is argued, this cannot normally happen.

It is legitimate, even at this stage of the development of team teaching, to try to distil from its theory and practice that which appears to be beneficial and successful and that which is still problematical; and experience so far points to some tentative conclusions:

1. If the movement towards team teaching in any school is too hasty there is a grave risk that the transition will be fraught with difficulties. In this respect it is comparable to the introduction of an Integrated Day. Where team teaching works really well, and where the transition has been smooth and comparatively trouble-free, reorganisation has been carried out slowly. Classes have been brought together a step at a time, perhaps for only one activity in one part of the day to begin with. As the change has been absorbed, and the necessary adjustments made by teachers as well as children, another step has been taken. In this way difficulties have been anticipated and avoided, or eradicated before they could have troublesome effects.

If the change, however, is too sudden the experience for the whole school can be disturbing and dissatisfying for months. This is a polite way of saying that the chaos and confusion can be quite appalling. It is like the Dark Ages. A flicker of learning may be kept alight in pockets here and there (only in bays instead of monasteries) but for a great many children it simply stops. Once confidence, control and organisation have broken down, it is a painful and uphill task to re-establish them and valuable time has been lost. No kind of organisation, however desirable in theory, justifies an experience of this kind, especially for children in the early years of their school lives.

2. There undoubtedly has to be a conscious professional adjustment on the part of the teacher from the independent to the joint responsibility. Her individuality does not have to be submerged, but it does have to operate within the limits of a united exercise. It is important that the need for this adjustment is acknowledged and accepted before any experiment in team

teaching begins or it will not flourish. On the other hand, if teachers find that they enjoy working together as members of a team, they do not appear to feel that their professional independence has been seriously threatened.

3. A thoughtful and really well planned structuring of the day seems to be essential if the aims of team teaching are to be fulfilled. There is little indication that the unstructured day which is sometimes tried has much chance of success. This means that the members of the team must meet regularly to reach agreement on strategy and to plan in detail, so that they all know what is expected of them and what their contribution to the team must be. Planning of this kind takes time, when all members of the team are free; and inevitably this is usually after school. There is no point at all in not being clear about a commitment which is almost certainly an essential element of good team teaching. Few infant teachers can regard themselves as free at the end of the school day, but there is a difference between preparation and planning which can mainly be done at home and that which unavoidably means staying on at school fairly regularly.

4. If a soundly organised Integrated Day, with family grouping, is already securely established the effective introduction of team teaching is incomparably easier. Indeed, it is difficult to see how a traditional teacher-directed programme can be smoothly adapted to anything more than a very pale representation of an organisation based on the collective contribution of members of a team and on the independent working of groups of children.

5. It is not always possible to overcome the physical limitations of schools designed rigidly on a single classroom plan. Although it is surprising how much can be done with buildings which at first sight look unpromising for team teaching, it remains a fact that there are schools which no amount of goodwill can alter successfully. If the design of the school imposes a genuine restriction on the manner in which a team could function, it is doubtful whether reorganisation would serve any very useful purpose.

In any educational experiment, the conviction and enthusiasm of those taking part in it are powerful factors in its success. No experiment can be judged by its outstanding successes or by its dismal failures. But both contribute to the experience on which sound educational innovation ultimately depends. At the centre of any innovation is the child, and in the infant school the child is young. His teacher, as a person, is very important to him. If she is a good teacher, he is in a happy position; if not, he cannot choose another, but at least she is someone whom he really knows. Both situations have a bearing upon team teaching. To return to the Plowden Report:

'We conclude that the class, with its own teacher, should remain the basic unit of school organisation, particularly for the younger children. The great bulk of teaching of children up to eight or nine should normally remain with the class teacher. Yet even at this age there are benefits in the children knowing and having access to other teachers. The classroom doors should no longer be shut, as still happens in some schools, with the teachers, both experienced and inexperienced, isolated in their rooms. . . . Inter-connecting classrooms and some shared working spaces can encourage teachers to make adjustments, to vary the size of groups for different purposes and to form some groups from more than one class.'[1]

Inconclusive and uncommitted this may be, and the enthusiast will doubtless condemn the compromise; but perhaps it is better to begin by paddling comfortably in shallow water than by diving in at the deep end before taking the precaution of learning to swim.

[1] Ibid., para. 772.

Chapter 10

Conclusion

Teaching methods, and the organisation which supports them, can never stand still. As society changes, so also do the needs and reactions of all its people, whatever their age. Psychological and sociological research inform us, over the years, about how children learn and what affects their capacity to do so. Teaching techniques must reflect this growth of knowledge, and the organisation of the school and the class must play their part. Yet however convincing the theoretical justification for change may be, it is in the classroom that the theory is tested and that its practical effects are judged. It is the children, first and foremost, who are affected by the results. In this, teachers bear a heavy responsibility. Too little change is stultifying; too much can create a vacuum, which is educationally unsound. It is on the balance between the two extremes that the progress and welfare of the children depend.

The organisation of a school has many objectives. One of these is unequivocal; the child must learn, and he must record what he has learned. All the discussion and the investigations about single-age or family grouping, Integrated Day, team teaching and the rest are arid unless the results are to the child's advantage. If any particular form of organisation does not help him to learn more effectively, more happily and to greater purpose, there is nothing whatever to be gained by imposing it upon him in the name of progressive education.

Throughout this book the point has been made that an organisational structure which works well in one set of circumstances does not necessarily work well in every other. There are too many variables in education for blanket solutions to be applied. There is only one valid criterion of any form of school organisation: *'Is it the best, at this moment of time, in this particular school?'* The possibility of future change is not denied. Circumstances alter, and experience grows. The door to change is never permanently shut. But there should be no mad rush to go through it because someone has said that the grass looks greener outside. To some children, it may be extraordinarily indigestible.

With modern methods, teaching, we believe, is better *but it is not easier*. Most important of all, it has not been abolished, even in the most old-fashioned sense of the word. There is danger in the myth that straightforward teaching has gone for ever from the educational scene, at least in the infant school. Because the teacher no longer stands in front of rows of silent infants, with a book in one hand and a piece of chalk in the other, it does not mean that she no longer teaches—directly and clearly.

It is not enough to supply children with books and material and equipment and to leave it to them to follow the paths of learning. Their own investigations, however exciting, and however much they share their discoveries with one another and with their teacher, are not, in themselves, sufficient. These things are unquestionably of the greatest importance, and they play a fundamental part in the educational environment of every child. But, in addition, the teacher must teach. She must *teach* them how to write, and how to read, and how to use their mathematical experience. She must systematise the results of their practical activity, so that it leads to solid advance.

It is vital to the success of modern methods that children should—in groups, individually, and even sometimes as a whole class—be given direct tuition. The Integrated Day is particularly subject to misinterpretation in this respect. In an earlier chapter it was defined as a form of organisation in which the child exercises a degree of choice about what he does and when he does it, and the teacher integrates his daily programme so that learning takes place. The word 'teaching' did not appear in the definition because it is unnecessary. If the teacher integrates the child's daily programme so that learning takes place, she cannot avoid teaching him. If she does not do so, learning will not take place.

Unhappily, however, it is sometimes implied that to take a child or a group of children for undisguised instruction, or indeed to direct their learning in any way, somehow violates the sacred principles of an Integrated Day. It cannot be said too often or too emphatically that teaching, both direct and indirect, is as important as ever it was, in any form of organisation. There is nothing in modern techniques which makes it superfluous. The difference is that with the individual approach it is not easy to teach, in the true sense of the word, without very good class management; and so the capacity to organise must now be included as an indispensable component of the infant teacher's professional skill. A well organised class, taught by good modern methods, has the critics of 'so-called progressive education' with their backs to the wall.

Select Bibliography

Blackie, John	*Inside the Primary School*, H.M.S.O., 1967.
Boyce, E. R.	*Play in the Infant School*, Methuen, 1948.
Boyce, E. R.	*The First Year in School*, Nisbet, 1953.
Boyce, E. R. (ed.)	*Today and Tomorrow*, (3 vols.) Macmillan, 1969.
Brown, Mary and Precious, Norman	*The Integrated Day in the Primary School*, Ward Lock Educational, 1968.
Gardner, D. E. M.	*Experiment and Tradition in Primary Schools*, Methuen, 1966.
Gardner, Dorothy E. M. and Cass, Joan E.	*The Role of the Teacher in the Infant and Nursery School*, Pergamon, 1965.
Mellor, Edna	*Education Through Experience in the Infant School Years*, Blackwell, 1950.
Plowden Report	*Children and Their Primary Schools*, H.M.S.O., 1967.
Ridgway, Lorna and Lawton, Irene	*Family Grouping in the Primary School*, Ward Lock Educational, 1968.
Sealey, L. G. W. and Gibbon, V.	*Communication and Learning in the Primary School*, Blackwell, 1962.
Sturmey, C. (ed.)	*Activity Methods for Children Under Eight*, Evans, 1949.
Walters, E. H.	*Activity and Experience in the Infant School*, National Froebel Foundation, 1963.

Index

Apparatus (card) or assignments: 24–33, 42–43, 63–65, 68, 89
  accessibility: 30–31, 71
  allocation of: 44
  grading: 28–30, 71
  introduction of new apparatus: 44–45
  presentation: 32
  reading and writing ability: 26–28
  reception class: 47–49
Assignments (see Apparatus)

Bays: 18–23, 31, 104, 106

Change of activity: 39–40
Change of occupation and physical position: 40, 42, 47
Classroom, organisation of: 15–23
Concentration, span of: 37–40
Control: 22, 55–56, 60, 62, 106
Corners (see Bays)
Cupboards, organisation of: 22–23

'Dayswork': 74–75
Delegation: 16, 22–23, 24–25, 28, 30, 35, 72
Direct teaching: 22, 44, 70, 72–73, 110–111
Discipline (see Control)

Grouping, of children within a class: 36–37, 42, 47, 60–61
Grouping, of classes within a school:
  family: 13, 35, 46, 59, 70, 91, 95–100, 107, 109
  parallel: 13, 46, 91, 98–100
  single-age: 13, 91–95, 97–100, 109

Integrated Day: 13, 34, 41, 51–57, 58–78, 79–82, 84, 89–90, 94, 97, 106–107, 109–111
  daily programmes: 63–65, 72–77, 81–82
  transition from traditional programme: 58–78

Marking: 88–90
Movement, limitation of: 41–43, 73

Plowden Report: 101, 108

Reading, hearing: 85–88
Reception class: 16, 38, 40, 46–50, 59, 85, 91–93
Records
  children's: 71, 83–85
  teacher's: 82–85
Room space, organisation of: 17–23, 41–43, 73

Teacher's attention: 45–46
Team teaching: 13, 101–108, 109
Traditional daily programme, organisation of: 34–50

Wall charts: 32–33
Wall pockets: 29–32
'Weekswork': 74–75, 77